Advance Praise for
# White Out: Understanding White Privilege and Dominance in the Modern Age

White people should read this important book. People of color who live near, work alongside, or otherwise interact with White persons will find much in this text that affirms their routine racialized experiences. Collins and Jun make smart sense of White dominance and help readers reimagine bold ways to disrupt it."

*Shaun R. Harper, Professor and Executive Director,*
*University of Southern California Race & Equity Center*

A meditation on race and ethnicity in the twenty-first century. Current. Thoughtful. Reflective. The authors place personal narratives in a larger context of what's happening, and what's not in the early decades of the twenty-first century."

*William G. Tierney, Wilbur Kieffer Professor of Higher Education,*
*University Professor & Co-director, Pullias Center for Higher Education,*
*University of Southern California*

# White Out

This book is part of the Peter Lang Education list.
Every volume is peer reviewed and meets
the highest quality standards for content and production.

PETER LANG
New York • Bern • Frankfurt • Berlin
Brussels • Vienna • Oxford • Warsaw

Christopher S. Collins and Alexander Jun

# White Out

## Understanding White Privilege
and Dominance
in the Modern Age

PETER LANG
New York • Bern • Frankfurt • Berlin
Brussels • Vienna • Oxford • Warsaw

**Library of Congress Cataloging-in-Publication Data**
Names: Collins, Christopher S., author. | Jun, Alexander, author.
Title: White out: understanding White privilege and dominance in the modern age /
Christopher S. Collins, Alexander Jun.
Description: New York: Peter Lang, 2017.
Includes bibliographical references and index.
Identifiers: LCCN 2016045992 | ISBN 978-1-4331-3541-5 (paperback: alk. paper)
ISBN 978-1-4331-4027-3 (ebook) | ISBN 978-1-4331-4028-0 (epub)
ISBN 978-1-4331-4029-7 (mobi) | DOI 10.3726/b10660
Subjects: LCSH: Whites—Race identity—United States.
Racism—United States. | Social stratification—United States.
Classification: LCC E184.A1 C538 2017 | DDC 305.800973—dc23
LC record available at https://lccn.loc.gov/2016045992

Bibliographic information published by **Die Deutsche Nationalbibliothek**.
**Die Deutsche Nationalbibliothek** lists this publication in the "Deutsche
Nationalbibliografie"; detailed bibliographic data are available
on the Internet at http://dnb.d-nb.de/.

We dedicate this book to our family and friends, who provided just the right amount of challenge and support we needed to accomplish this worthwhile endeavor.

For Kristy, Mateo, and Adela:
May we be peacemakers, justice-seekers, and messengers.
—Christopher S. Collins

For Jeany, Natalia, Isaiah, and Jeremiah:
Do justice. Love mercy. Walk humbly.
—Alexander Jun

Lastly, we would like to dedicate this work to the Social Justice and Diversity Fellowship recipients at the Ph.D. program in higher education program at Azusa Pacific. All of the proceeds from this publication will go to enhance the fellowship program to support students pursuing doctoral studies and pursing social justice.

# Contents

# Figures

# Acknowledgments

This book was born out of tension, agony, excavation, and longing. Over the past decade, we taught doctoral courses, spoke at college campuses around the country, and conducted workshops for faculty, staff, and students on issues related to diversity and racial justice in higher education.

This book was the result of deep self-excavation and refection. We had to examine our own logic, suspend judgment at times, cultivate our own vulnerability without becoming fragile, and find new terrains of cultural humility. Throughout most of our interactions, we have heard some recurring objections, rebuttals, and arguments from students and colleagues at all levels within the academy. It was through these conversations that we sought to develop new language in an attempt to reshape well-established concepts. We undertook this task in order to articulate more clearly what we have heard mostly from folks in the dominant White majority.

We are indebted to the many colleagues who have dialoged with us, especially to our graduate students who have continuously pressed us to think more deeply about issues of systemic racism, power, privilege, and dominance.

In the midst of a plethora of national events, tragedies, and tense dialogues surrounding race relations these past few years, we felt provoked. In the midst of teaching class and conducting research, we watched students of color share deeply immense stories of pain and hurt. These stories were juxtaposed by White students whose responses could be described as ambivalent, silently resistant, or awkward entry these conversations. Again, we felt committed. As we wrote furiously into 2016, the events kept pouring in, our curriculum kept re-writing itself, and we came to a point where we knew this would be unfinished business; instead, that we would cement our imperfection in a final copy.

Figure A. August 2015 when we decided to begin writing this project, we passed a community chess game and ultimately agreed that it was "Whites Turn" to be the subject of a justice project.

The work we have done has been immensely influenced by writers and thinkers from all over the world. We cite many of them throughout the book, but we list a few here in the foreword, not only to give them credit, but to encourage our readers to embrace these authors as well. Shaun Harper's work in higher education has not only been informative but inspiriting and his new book, *Race Matters in College* will be essential reading in our class and in our future projects. Lori Patton and Nolan Cabrera have written extensively on issues of Whiteness that form an empirical and sound backdrop to the work we present here. In the earlier stages of our career, we have been deeply transformed by the work of William Tierney, Sylvia Hurtado, Mitch Chang, Darryl Smith, and Walter Allen. In the earliest stages of our formation, we are deeply indebted to Cornel West, Henry Louis Gates Jr., William Julius Wilson, Alan Paton, James Cone, Paolo Freire, and Ada Maria Isasi Diaz. We appreciate the support of Race and Justice in Higher Education research assistants Jennifer Akamine Phillips, Redgina Hill, Gyasmine George-Williams, Sharia Hays, Greg Veltman, Monica Johnson, Mari Luna De La Rosa, and Kelly Montz. We are also thankful for good friends and colleagues who are invested in this work in a way that goes way beyond our ability, including Julie Park, Sam Museus, Frank Harris III, Kimberly Griffin, Darnell Cole, Oiyan Poon, Tracy Lachica Buenavista, Liliana Graces, Victor Saenz, Ryiad Shanjahan, and many others.

We found our thoughts to be in a continuous stage of formation and in need of review, input, and challenge to make the project accessible to as many people as possible. We are so deeply grateful for Kristin Paredes-Collins and her willingness to read every word of this book and translate it for clarity of concepts and syntax. Tabatha Jones Jolivet is an intellectual activist and an amazing colleague who helped us to see our blind spots in so many areas. We appreciate colleagues who have offered feedback to various drafts of chapters, including Allison Ash, Joe Slavens, Nate Risdon, Jody Wiley Fernando, and Rukshan Fernando.

We are thankful for the support of Laurie Schreiner, chair of the department of higher education, and for Bob Welsh, dean of the school of behavioral and applied sciences at Azusa Pacific University. As this work is a collaborative and communal effort in the search for justice, we recognize those who have come before us and those will follow.

If you are interested in following current updates on events and research in higher education as it relates to diversity, you can visit the Race and Justice in Higher Education website (rjhe.org) to learn more about the research and education collaborative that produces and curates resources about racial justice for the improvement of higher education. You can also follow the collaborative on twitter (@raceNjustice) and Facebook (www.facebook.com/rjhe.org).

# Chapter One

# Introduction: The White Architecture of the Mind

## White Out

A doctoral student at a university in the southern half of the US was set to be one of the first Black graduates of his PhD program. He often outperformed his peers with academic achievements and was given honors for his efforts on completing his doctoral examinations. However, on one occasion after writing an exam in a standard blue book, his advisor responded to one answer in red ink with the comment, "*N[word] you know better.* This is to show you that race had nothing to do with your grade." The student went on to perform at the top level of the program and upon graduation his advisor proclaimed his role in the success of the first Black graduate of the program. He built a successful career, but always kept that exam. In some ways, the comment attacked his mind and sense of self, and in other ways it motivated him. One day, the newly minted PhD used Wite-Out, the name brand correction liquid, to cover up the comment, but left the blue book in his desk. A few years later, students and fellow professors challenged the veteran professor for being insensitive and even racist. The professor went to see his former student to talk to him about these attacks and look for support and testimony that he was not a *racist*. The former student listened and then pulled out the old exam that he wrote in a blue book. He showed the professor the incendiary comment written years earlier, but the professor could not see it—the Wite-Out had covered up the comment. Because the professor could not see it through the Wite-Out, the student turned to all of the consecutive indented pages to show him the words that could be seen and felt because of the indentation. In spite of an attempt to blot out the words written in the blue book and the effect on his life, the indention went deep into the pages and perhaps into the psyche of the lives of students subjected to this kind of interaction.

We use this story to help frame the concept of White Out as strategy or habit that serves to defend White dominance in a multicultural age. It is the notion that attempts to cover systems, dispositions, and actions cannot cover the full indentation or impact. White Out, the action of intentional or unintentional blotting, serves the purpose of trying to obscure others experiences in lieu of a competing definition of reality. The degree to which an experience can be denied creates room for a dominant conception to be defined as reality.[1] White Out is also a weather term for when a blizzard or a snow covered horizon combined with light reduces visibility to almost zero. Both standard definitions serve to use the concept as social, race-based, and largely unconscious strategy to reinforce White dominance.

## Social Construction

This book is about the role of Whiteness in a diverse society. *Whiteness* is a socially constructed status that is often assumed to be biological as it relates to skin color. Race is undoubtedly a social construct, as various periods in history show that Whiteness was an achievable status. For example, consider the Italians and Irish as early immigrants to the US and their ability to achieve a generically White status, while Africans who were forced to immigrate under slavery were given the socially constructed status of 3/5 of a human being.[2] We define Whiteness as a system. There are many discussions about pscyho-social attitudes on race, and while we address those, we are predominately concerned with a larger system that has constructed such a dominant reality that it narrows our sense of choices and beliefs as it relates to race. The systems in which we live and operate can be compared to architecture, or a design that creates limited choices one can make when it comes to moving into certain spaces, opening doors, staying, or departing.

Consider the fable of the giraffe and the elephant.[3] A giraffe is the cornerstone of the fable and he has just completed a house. It was a perfect house for his family's specifications. It had high windows, which allowed for privacy and lots of light. It had narrow hallways, which allowed for maximum use of space in a convenient passageway. The perfectly designed house was the pride of the neighborhood and won national awards for its design. When the giraffe was working in his shop one day, he looked out the window and saw an elephant he knew that was also a woodworker. Much to the delight of the elephant, the giraffe invited him in to see the woodshop. After small talk, they encountered a problem in that the elephant could only get his head in the doorway. The giraffe noted that it was not a problem because extra doors had been designed to accommodate his woodshop equipment and so the elephant was able to get inside. While talking about woodworking, the giraffe's wife called from upstairs to indicate the giraffe needed to talk to his supervisor on the phone. The giraffe told the elephant he had to go upstairs and that it might take a while, so to make himself at home. After sometime, the elephant thought he better go upstairs to see what is happening and ended up causing damage to the stairs, the walls, and the décor. The giraffe came to see the commotion and asked what the elephant was doing, and he said he was making himself at home. The giraffe suggested that if he takes some aerobic classes he might be able to slim down and fit through the passageways and not cause so much damage to the stairs. The elephant responded that a house designed for a giraffe might never work for an elephant.

The recognizable application to diverse groups of people occupying the same space conveys that much of reality (or architecture) is designed to be the best fit for one group. Because it is a dominant reality, any group for whom the architecture does not work, it is the fault of the persons in that group—an individual problem that could be adjusted by assimilating. From our perspective, the giraffe house represents the systemic Whiteness that permeates the US and even larger global sense of reality. Fables and analogies fail to represent the full complexity of the subject matter. For example, the giraffe and the elephant story does not capture the long history between giraffes and elephants, the disparate generational sources of wealth, and the ongoing denial of any difference in a post civil rights era. It goes much deeper than physical space or even policy environments to create what we call the White architecture of the mind. Similar to physical architecture that restricts and guides action and the available choices individuals are able to make and the degree to which groups can interaction, the White architecture of the mind restricts and guides choices, reactions, and responses.

One aspect of mental architecture is to understand where thinking occurs as either fast or slow.[4] Thinking fast is another way of describing automatic and reactionary thoughts. For example, when reading the problem 2+2, it is virtually impossible to avoid generating the answer. However, when reading the problem 14×37, additional labor may be required to generate the answer. Even if given multiple-choice options, the answer may not be readily discernable indicating that one must think more slowly to generate the answer. In the Muller-Lyer illusion, two parallel lines are shown with the question of which is longer.

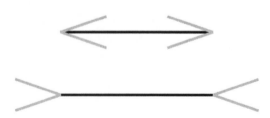

Figure 1.1. Muller-Lyer Illusion[5]

The typical way the human eye and brain connection interprets the illusion is that the bottom line, with arrows pointing out, is shorter than the top line. Precise measurement, however, shows the lines to be the exact same length, in spite of what the typical visual-mental response is to the illusion. However, upon seeing the illusion for the second time, even if it looks like the bottom line is shorter, when asked the question, people will respond that they are the same length. This is a rewiring of the brain—a new space in the mental architecture to respond to tricks or illusions. In our classes, we use an alternate version of the illusion where the bottom line is in fact shorter to see how students respond. Students typically indicate that they are the same length, which highlights how thinking slow becomes thinking fast and leaves responses vulnerable to similar mistakes.

## Implicit Bias

Applications of thinking fast or reacting automatically in diverse groups of people are related to the notion of implicit bias. Project Implicit, based at Harvard University, offers the Implicit Association Test (IAT). The Project claims that the test measures attitudes and beliefs that people may be unwilling or unable to report, and that:

> The IAT may be especially interesting if it shows that you have an implicit attitude that you did not know about. For example, you may believe that women and men should be equally associated with science, but your automatic associations could show that you (like many others) associate men with science more than you associate women with science.[6]

The test uses fast thinking to uncover imbedded or implicit value constructs about a variety of identities. The test filters implicit thinking by examining strength of associations between concepts (e.g., black people, gay people) and evaluations (e.g., good, bad) or stereotypes (e.g., athletic, clumsy). Responses come more quickly or easily when closely related items share the same response key. In the 1940s, Clark and Clark conducted the famous doll study that revealed both White and Black children show preferences for lighter skin.[7] The study was used in the Brown v. Board of Education case about segregation and was recreated on a small scale by child psychologist and University of Chicago professor Margaret Beale Spencer. The 2010 study found that white children have a high rate of white bias and that black children also have white bias at a lower rate. Spencer also found that racial attitudes do not evolve as children grown older.[8] Thinking slow, or effortfully provides the opportunity to rewire automatic responses, which is required to compete with the implicit or unconscious mental architecture that guides decision-making.

The White architecture of the mind is a term and an analogy to highlight that the mind is a result of a set of blueprints, constructions, walls, doors, windows, and pathways that influence and predispose individuals to react based on a systemic logic that was socially constructed. Put differently, we use the term to indicate the individual actions, choices, behaviors, and attitudes that are guided by a socially constructed system that predisposes these attitudes and grants privileges and accessibilities to core members of a dominant group. For example, if someone chooses a house in a gated neighborhood with a particular style and level of prestige, it may be reasonable to think it was all a matter of individual choice and fit. However, there was a system of priming effects that conditioned the individual to be attracted to a particular style and a system of builders, city codes, and Home Owners Association regulations that led to the creation of the neighborhood, in addition to the segmented way populations group together based on race and income. That system and all of its components create an architecture of the mind, and when it goes unrecognized, decisions are thought to be of individual volition for the rational mind. Similar to the ongoing nurture vs. nature debate in the social and natural sciences, there is an individual vs. systemic debate in the quest for explaining society's largely disparate outcomes when it comes to income, wealth, education, standardized test scores, employment, and crime rates that are all divided along racial lines. Is it a matter of individuals needing to make choices, or is society directed by a social construction built upon White privilege?

Take for example, a White person engaging in direct social action to combat racism. Imagine this person to be familiar with intercultural terminology and to be well educated. Privilege may be acknowledged, but not racism, as that is often assumed to be an individual attitude and corresponding set of actions. Trying to understand the deeply imbedded impact of racism becomes difficult in the case of such an individual because his or her overt actions are not racist and it is difficult to show that someone is a racist. As a result, bell hooks shifted from using racism to talk about White supremacy as a means to understand the social structure that creates pervasive oppression. She wrote,

> When liberal whites fail to understand how they can and/or do embody white supremacist values and beliefs even though they may not embrace racism ... they cannot recognize the ways their actions support and affirm the very structure or racist domination and oppression that they wish to see eradicated.[9]

By using hooks notion of White supremacy, we also try to focus on how a White architecture is essential to defending White dominance.

A more personal example of the White architecture of the mind is when I (Collins) was listening to a long awaited decision that emerged out of Ferguson, Missouri following the shooing of Michael Brown. Officer Darren Wilson shot and killed Brown, an unarmed 18 year old black man who had just engaged in petty theft at a convenient store. The details of the story were varied and unclear, but no one disputed that this young man was unarmed, and it was clear the city had a long history of racially polarizing habits and an unequal application of the law between black and white citizens.[10] Following the previous death of Trayvon Martin and countless other individuals in US history, I found myself provoked by the news stories. It was unimaginable that George Zimmerman was not convicted for killing Trayvon Martin, and now a police officer was making global news for killing a young Michael Brown. The decision on whether or not officer Wilson would be indicted was delayed several times, but was finally delivered on November 24, 2014. I sat watching the television with angst, prepared to feel offense by the lack of action that seemed destined to follow. As the details of the case were described, it was clear that a decision not to indict was about to be delivered. As I listened to the details of the case unfold, my disdain dissipated and my offense was nowhere to be found. Instead, I found myself thinking, this is a well thought out, thoroughly investigated, tough to dispute, and a reasonable decision. Then, I went back to social media outlets to observe the explosion of comments and eventually went to bed for the night with the implicit knowledge that this decision would not impact my immediate or future life.

As I (Collins) reflect on my experience and the divergence between what I expected to feel and actually felt, I attribute the deeply ingrained White architecture of my mind as the reason for my response. Part of the original blueprints for my mental architecture includes that police officers are public servants that are part of a system that protects, not executes people. Part of my original understanding of reality is that all people, regardless of race and class, have opportunities to achieve. If they are good people, work hard, and do the right things, they will achieve a comfortable life often referred to as the upwardly mobile *American Dream*. Much of these original plans for my mental architecture had been dismantled as a sociology major in my undergraduate studies. Courses about social stratification, race, and the nature of reality retooled my understanding of the world. In reflecting on my response to the decision for Officer Wilson, it is a poignant reminder that even when architecture is modified or replaced, you can still find remnants of its influence—even in unexpected ways. For a moment in time, the White architecture of my mind enabled me to comfortably White Out the raw pain I saw entire communities experiencing and to allow the dominant narrative to explain them away.

Juxtapose my (Collins) response to the writing of Ta-Nehisi Coates. In his book, "Between the World and Me," which is written as a letter to his teen-age son, Coates shares about his own emotional struggles as a father having to explain to his child why Michael Brown's murderer was set free. In explaining why there would be no trial, and in many ways a direct contradiction to my own White architecture, Coates revealed the Black architecture that captures the essence of what it means to be Black in White America—to live in constant fear of disembodiment; that the Black body is targeted for destruction, and is thus in a constantly vulnerable state. For Coates then, from his Black architectural perspective, police officers may merely be part of a White supremacist system that exist to protect and serve White citizens, but regularly execute Black citizens with impunity. His perspective and his reaction, along with the responses of countless other people of color in light of the non-verdict, reveals a profound difference in ontological assumptions and the resulting interpretations and reactions as a result of disparate Black and White architectures of the mind.

## Dominance Beyond Whiteness

When presenting this framework to a group of colleagues, a White female was the first to ask a question—"Do you distinguish between White males and females?" It was an appropriate first question given the complexity of multidimensional intersectionality imbedded within a socially constructed reality.[11] The question points back to the root of social arrangements around power where dominance is also coupled with being male, cisgender, straight, a US citizen, middle or upper class, and many other identity realities. We acknowledge and identify the importance of these constructed power arrangements and the additional complexity that comes with intersections. Our approach is about race, racism, and Whiteness, not in an attempt to leave out other realities (or worse, blot them out), but to focus on a version of dominance that will remain incomplete when devoid of context. We also find it important to highlight the ways in which intersectionality can be exploited. Indeed, we find the strongest defense of White dominance is a deflection of Whiteness onto some other status that is used to mitigate the benefit associated with being White.

We ask the reader to consider your own positionality in relation to social realities. Intersecting identities and being multicontextual is a fixed aspect of many folks who live and have lived in the reality of "double consciousness," as coined by Du Bois,[12] but also the multiple consciousness that people of color, women, queer folk, and others who don't have the privilege of functioning in the single reality driven by White dominance. Our consciousness demands a vision of multiple realities and we advocate for an expanding consciousness through decolonization, because we are subject to internalizing Whiteness and other forms of dominance (even though only one of us is White). The perpetuation of White dominance is not simply about White identity, but is a project in which minoritized peoples play a role. Internalized oppression can reinforce the White architecture of the mind.

Many of the examples we give and our own reflections are rooted in a Black-White binary. Similar to other issues of intersectionality, we do not intend for this to be the whole of the conversation. I (Collins) am White and I (Jun) am Korean, Asian-American, and we find that the Black-White binary is an important starting point for understanding the dominance of White systems and how they are perpetuated, but certainly not the end. The White architecture of the mind, the history of Whiteness, and the strategies to maintain dominance are key theoretical components of our argument.

## Higher Learning

We are also university professors, and many of our examples throughout the book are about college campuses. Although we hope that our location in higher education does not preclude the concepts from being applicable in many other situations, we also found that higher education is a contested space where a lot of conversations around diversity and Whiteness are located. Conversations about diversity in higher education and in various segments of the workforce are often concerned with predominant Whiteness or predominately White institutions (PWIs). The notion of predominance is in reference to ratios. Any segment of an organized body that is 51% White is predominately white. In higher education, for example, many institutions are in a rush to achieve 51% non-whiteness. Institutions are so committed to achieving a non-PWI status, there are numerous court cases and legislation emerging year after year about the ability and the degree to which race can be used as some kind of criteria in college admission.[13] Institutions that are far from achieving this 51% status start by claiming victory with a new class of students that is 51% or more nonwhite. The federal government is offering funding for institutions that have a certain percentage of Latin@ students after applying to become a Hispanic Serving Institution (HSIs). We find the term PWI and the focus on ratios of students to be a weak unit of analysis. For the purposes of this book, we focus more on dominant whiteness and Dominantly White Institutions (DWIs), which accounts for the history, location, habits, and proportions of faculty and executives who are White.[14] Focusing on dominant as opposed to predominate Whiteness creates a framework in which mental architecture and strategies to blot out counter stories and deny privilege become pertinent to understanding diversity.

Higher education is a place where inequality and diversity collide as institutions engage in various methods to expand critical consciousness. The events recounted about Trayvon Martin who died in 2012 and Michael Brown who died in August 2014 have been surrounded by a number of highly publicized events. Just before Brown was shot, Eric Garner was killed by a police officer who used an illegal chokehold while Garner repeatedly said, "I can't breathe." After Garner and Brown, a young 12-year-old Tamir Rice was shot by police officers that mistook his toy for a weapon. Eric Harris was shot and killed in April 2015 when a reserve officer grabbed his gun instead of a police taser. Walter Scott was killed two days later while running away from a traffic stop. The video footage shows him being shot while running away. Freddie Gray died of spinal cord injuries only two weeks later because of injuries suffered in a police van. In October 2014, 17-year-old Laquan McDonald was shot 16 times (9 times in the back) and killed by police in Chicago, but it took 13 months for the video to be released. In July 2015, Sandra Bland was pulled over for a traffic stop that escalated and lead to her arrest where she died in jail three days later. In addition to these police killings of unarmed black men, women, and children, numerous videos of police removing black minors from classrooms, intervening in quarrels, and disbanding neighborhood parties have surfaced and demonstrated an aggressive level of force. The Black Lives Matter movement started after a collection of these events catalyzed a sense of activism around the United States. Most of what we just chronicled are tragic encounters between Whiteness and Black men and boys. The violence against Black women goes way beyond the death of Sandra Bland, but much of the violence remains invisible as documented by the *Say Her Name* project out of Columbia Law School.[15] Mya Hall was a Black transgender woman who was killed in 2015 in Baltimore after taking the wrong exit and approaching an NSA building; she was shot and died after crashing into the gate. In contrast to the killings of Eric Garner and Freddie Gray, this incidence was written off as involving someone who had a troubled past, which may have served to overlook the fact that police killed an unarmed Black woman.

A particular concern for our project is the counter sayings to the Black Lives Matter movement: All Lives Matter and Blue Lives Matter (in reference to police). We discuss these responses in greater detail in chapter two. On university campuses across the country, the Black Lives Matter movement garnered support and catalyzed activism and protest as students felt more compelled to outline their experience at Dominantly White Institutions (DWIs). The activism came to a climax in November 2015 at the University of Missouri where racial tensions had been growing, a student began a hunger strike, and the football team refused to play until the president resigned. Concurrently, protests took place at Yale University over emails about Halloween costumes, sensitivity, and faculty/staff support, and the student body president and Dean of Students at Claremont McKenna stepped down over similarly embattled issues.

## Volume 1 and Beyond

The White responses that exhibit the principles of White Out are included throughout the chapters of this book. White student violence, threats of violence, and taunting increased exponentially at the University of Missouri and other places. At a Christian college in the Midwest, a student drew the Nazi symbol in the snow on cars in a parking lot, and a White President at a DWI wrote a letter to the student body explaining that the university is not a day care or a safe place and if students are too sensitive they should attend elsewhere. Reports of professors using racial slurs in the classroom increased and claims to academic freedom and the oversensitivity of students were used as a canopy to protect the sacredness of being able to unintentionally demean students of color. The combined weight of these events and many more are the backdrop in which White Out can be examined as an intentional or unintentional strategy to blot out the counter stories of people of color who live on the margins or the outside of the socially constructed dominant White reality.

There are a variety of ways in which White Out can be applied as a byproduct of mental architecture. The often-unconscious purpose in denying privilege and articulating colorblind sameness is to support a larger system and view of reality. The first strategy is about claims to pain in a systemic effort to communicate a sameness of experience regardless of race or details. Chapter two, entitled *White Pain*, includes an important distinction between pain that is caused by a system that predisposes certain populations to suffer as opposed to more randomized acts of violence that likely occur without respect to race. This distinction is a difficult one to make, because pain is personal; however, that is why claims to be in pain become a volatile White Out strategy that avoids the systemic nature of dominant Whiteness.

Chapter three, *Whitefluenza: Privilege is an epidemic with no cure*, outlines the ever elusive, incurable, virus-like veracity of privilege in a world built on generational wealth, entitlements, and trickle up economics (the rich are getting richer and the poor are getting poorer). When going to the doctor for advice or treatment about symptoms that feel like the common cold, a bacterial infection yields the often sought after antibiotics, and a viral infection yields the sad realization that the patient must wait out the symptoms. A virus is a microscopic infectious agent that replicates and mutates inside of other living organisms. A virus can spread in many different ways and survive in modular particles when not infecting a host, and antibiotics have no impact. Sometimes it remains dormant for extended periods of time, only to flare up at critical moments to once again sustain the equilibrium of privilege for those in a dominant position. For some viruses, a healthy immune system can eliminate them, or vaccines can inoculate a host from being infected. Privilege acts in many of the same ways in promoting and protecting dominant whiteness and often operates more effectively when undetected or acknowledged.

Drawing from more of the developmental and individual perspective of whiteness, chapter four, *White 22*, which plays off of Joseph

Heller's novel Catch 22, addresses the no-win situations that many white individuals are confronted with daily. There is a great deal of tension between the threat of inactivity in the face of injustice and the liabilities associated with active anti-racist activity that can actually be harmful due to unintended consequences. This chapter explores the evolving role and perception on whiteness and the desire for right action in the face of a long history of dominance. White 22 is a term that refers to the "White if you do or White if you don't" tension that exists when White advocates engage in anti-racist activity.

Chapter five, which we have entitled *Whitrogressions*, explores negative attitudes and microaggressions toward whiteness and even white individuals to unpack the role of power and dominance in racist systems and actions. Derogatory racial slurs toward White people and people of color are often perceived differently, but claims of reverse racism function as an attempt to eliminate claims of asymmetry. In this chapter, we highlight emerging depictions of being White in popular culture and in art, including an overview of whether or not the term douche bag is a long awaited White racial slur with more poignancy than honkey or cracker. Some White responses to criticism rely on using the same language as people of color, which combined with stealing pain, serves to White Out the reality of asymmetrical experiences. Thus the term Whitrogressions is an important concept that is akin to microaggressions—subtle and cumulative slights against minority identities that are often more acceptable than overt expressions of racism.

In chapter six, *Angry White Men: Making America Great Again*, we turn to the palpable anger that accompanies the evolution from privilege to equality, which can feel like oppression. This anger is highlighted by events like the Oregon standoff with the Bundy brothers, the energy behind the Donald Trump presidential campaign, and the continued discontent on college campuses where White Student Unions have emerged, and affirmative action bake sales continue. In order to extract some sense of dispositional and behavioral shifts resulting from notions of pain claims, Whitefluenza, White 22, and Whitrogressions, chapter seven, *White Pilgrims* is about the interactions White people have within their White communities and the ways in which speech patterns and reactions reflect or react against a dominant white mental architecture.

The concluding chapter, *Good White Friends*, is a more conceptual guide for understanding White identity, grounded in prevailing literature on whiteness. We outline the history and progression of White identity development theories, including the work of Janet Helms, Rowe, Bennett, and Atkinson's conceptualization on White consciousness. We identify potential gaps in the corpus of literature on white identity and introduce our models of critical white consciousness, as well as a conceptual model of the awareness-engagement continuum. The purpose of this concluding chapter is to offer some constructive ideas on how the notion of being a White ally and recognizing the evolution of White identity may play a role in shifting dominant White systems through consciousness and decolonization.

Although this volume is a brief introduction to contemporary notions of Whiteness that have been constructed over centuries, there are subsequent follow up volumes in consortium with this project that are currently en route. The first, *White Jesus*, considers the role of Whiteness in religion at large, but primarily Christianity. The notion of a White Jesus is perhaps one of the key constructs of a White system that was cultivated in Europe and exported around the globe. History, religion, and the knowledge producing capabilities of churches and Christian universities will be key elements of this volume.

The third volume in this project is entitled, *Global White Southerner*. In the US, someone from the South is anything South of the Mason Dixon line and is associated with a particular history and culture. The state of Texas is not even considered the true South by some in states like Georgia and Alabama. From an international perspective, the global South refers primarily to countries South of the equator, which include regions like sub-Saharan Africa, Southeast Asia, and portions of South America, which contain some of the poorest regions of the world when measured by the Human Development Index. However, the geographic territory of the global South also includes New Zealand, Australia, South Africa, and Zimbabwe. White persons in these countries confound the typical Western notions and issues of Whiteness. White

Afrikaaners and White Rhodesians are still a dominant White minority in the Southern portion of the continent. White persons in Australia are considered involuntary colonizers due to the history of their placement on the continent and consequently have a very different approach (or lack thereof) to identity and consciousness around Whiteness. The collection of global Southern White perspectives will offer more insights into a world system of Whiteness that spread over centuries through movements of people groups, ideas, knowledge systems, and domination.

## Notes

1. Berger, Peter L., Thomas Luckmann, and Dariuš Zifonun. *The social construction of reality*. New York: Random House, na, 2002.

   *The Social Construction of Reality*, is particularly informative as is it conveys a framework in which dominant views of reality attempt to assimilate or annihilate competing views of reality. A perspective becomes dominant through a process of habituation and legitimation and is then conferred as reality. The notion that it is socially constructed points to the fact that it can be created and destroyed and does not have an objective and value neutral status. It is still a reality because it influences how people think and behave, and it positions themselves in relationship to the structure that supports that reality.

2. Roediger, David R. *Working toward whiteness: How America's immigrants became white: The strange journey from Ellis Island to the suburbs*. New York: Basic Books, 2006. For more on this topic, see Roediger's book, which outlines the legal process for Dagos and Wasps becoming White and the economic effects it had on other immigrant groups with darker skin tones.

3. Thomas, Roosevelt R., and Marjorie I. Woodruff. *Building a house for diversity*. New York: AMACOM, 1999. The book begins with this fable that sets the stage for applying to diversity in various contexts.

4. Kahneman, Daniel. *Thinking, fast and slow*. London: Macmillan, 2011. Kahneman's work is a thorough and empirical look at two general ways of thinking.

5. Müller-Lyer, Franz Carl. Optische Urteilstäuschungen. *DuboisReymonds Archiv für Anatomie und Physiologie*, Supplement Volume, 1889. 263–270.

6. "Project Implicit". Accessed September 20, 2015, https://implicit.harvard.edu/implicit/education.html.

7. Kenneth, B., and Mamie P. Clark. "Racial Identification and Preference in Negro Children." *Readings in Social Psychology* 19, no. 3 (1950): 341–350.

8. "White and black children biased toward lighter skin," *CNN.com*, last modified May 14, 2010, http://www.cnn.com/2010/US/05/13/doll.study/.
9. hooks, bell. *Talking back: Thinking feminist, thinking black*. South End Press, 1989, 113.
10. Matt, Apuzzo. "Ferguson Police Routinely Violate Rights of Blacks, Justice Department Finds," *New York Times*, last modified March 3, 2015, http://www.nytimes.com/2015/03/04/us/justice-department-finds-pattern-of-police-bias-and-excessive-force-in-ferguson.html?_r=1
11. Hill-Collins, Patricia, and Sirma Bilge. *Intersectionality*. John Wiley & Sons, 2016, 2. We draw from the following definition of intersectionality: "When it comes to social inequality, people's lives and the organizations of power in a given society are better understood as being shaped not by a single axis of social division, be it race or gender or class, but by many axes that work together and influence each other. Intersectionality as an analytic tool gives people better access to the complexity of the world and of themselves."
12. Du Bois, William Edward Burghardt, and Brent Hayes Edwards. *The souls of black folk*. Oxford: Oxford University Press, 2008.
13. *Fisher v The University of Texas* (II) is the latest, but was preceded by Gratz v and Grutter v Bollinger at the University of Michigan. The general rule is that it can be loosely applied but not as a major criteria.
14. Gusa, Diane Lynn. "White institutional presence: The impact of Whiteness on campus climate." *Harvard Educational Review* 80, no. 4 (2010): 464–490. See more about the notion of White Institutional Presence (WIP) for more about the culture of a campus and the way it includes or excludes various epistemologies and ideologies.
15. Crenshaw, Kimberlé, Andrea J. Ritchie, Rachel Anspach, Rachel Gilmer, and Luke Harris. *Say her name: Resisting police brutality against black women*. New York: The African American Policy Forum, 2015.

# Chapter Two

# White Pain: I Hurt Too

As we have traveled to college campuses around the country engaging in conversations on racial justice over the years, we have noticed an interesting phenomenon that often occurs when White people engage in discussions about racism alongside people of color. As people of color begin to share real life experiences and examples of systemic racism—a discussion that can implicate White systems built by faculty, administrators, and students—White people often respond to racialized pain with their own stories of hurt, pain, suffering, and loss. We acknowledge that systems of racism tie together the pain of the oppressor and oppressed.[1] However, we have found that White pain and further identification with other systems of dominance based on identity markers around gender, class, ability status can be used as an attempt to delegitimize the pain that people of color endure within the systems of racialized oppression.

White pain is a pattern of how White folks either unwittingly or with passive aggressive defense strategies place their own pain in the foreground of a discussion to the exclusion and erasure of pain that racialized others face. Applying White Out to explanations of racial pain simultaneously denies and defends the dominant structure. I (Jun) recall a particularly heated exchange when a White male colleague, after hearing several other colleagues share emotional stories of racism and misogyny, voiced his concern to the group. He blurted aloud, as his faced slowly turned crimson, "I hurt too!" He went on to share how he was robbed and the assailants were never charged, tried, or convicted. His personal pain was very real, very devastating, and worthy of empathy and compassion. Yet, I could not help but wonder if the "I hurt too" trope also functions in discussions like this as a way of diffusing White responsibility in the face of systemic racialized pain. In other words, not all pain is the same.

In conversations about racial injustice, pain claims are never neutral. What does it mean to steal down another's pain? How do we deal with the realities of white pain when navigating conversations about race and racism? What are the motivations behind the need to share a story of deep personal pain in response to stories of systemic racism? Moreover, what is the impact of these responses that ultimately serve to defend White dominance in the face of racialized pain? We offer this exchange as one of many examples we (Jun and Collins) have encountered with our White students and colleagues, as well as what is regularly argued on social media. The observable pattern demonstrates that White logic programs a response to recollections of racism with own stories of individual pain, family alcoholism, divorce, weight gain, or childhood bullying. Although we seek to understand intent, we know that the impact is ultimately an erasure and negation of the pain people of color systematically face, which is an extended defense of White dominance.

A central tenet of Critical Race Theory (CRT) is idea of intent versus impact.[2] The intersecting nature of intent and impact is a fundamental justice issue. If a grocery store patron knocks over a person with a cart and offers as an explanation, "I did not mean to hurt you," does not change the damage that transpired. Similarly, if the offender immediately begins telling a story about when they were knocked down or hurt in some way, it does not change the impact of that event. Even worse, offering an explanation about standing in the middle of the aisle as opposed to the side of the aisle would exacerbate the pain. "I apologize if you were hurt while standing in my way" is no apology. When people say or do something that is racist, sexist, or homophobic, they often defend their motivation and divorce their impact from intent. At some point, the intent does not matter as much as the impact. White pain claims in response to hearing stories of racialized pain and injustice should be evaluated through the lens of impact more than intent.

Initially, our simplistic assessment of these perplexing responses was that expressing White pain was rooted in assessing the psychological need to shift the conversation away from the burden of White guilt. In truth, there are an infinite number of motivations for these types of responses, and indeed what might be at work is far more complex. Perhaps it could be a disappointment that the mythical promise of White supremacy has not been fulfilled. Perhaps that, in addition to turning away from guilt, White pain, as legitimate as it is, might also be deployed as a strategy to diffuse responsibility for being complicit in systems of inter-structured oppression. Our point is that White pain, when used in this way, can serve to erase the systems of pain at work in the lives of people of color and that Whites systematically benefit from this erasure, irrespective of intent. While it is true that sharing painful stories can be an attempt to join in solidarity with the pain of racialized "others," it is also true that the impact of "I hurt too" responses is rooted in denying others' pain. Consequently, stating that they have had it worse, Whites ultimately convey to people of color that they should stop complaining. We explore some of these responses and motivations a little deeper in the following section.

## Empathy and Solidarity

Often, the work of diversity, equity, and inclusion emphasizes the role of empathy and solidarity. A generous interpretation of White pain as a response to racialized oppression may signal attempts at genuine caring and support. In other words, the "I hurt too" response can be an attempt at solidarity. For example, when Black colleagues share a difficult racialized experience, White colleagues might want to be empathetic to their colleague. The "I hurt too" response can be about joining with the humanity of another. If White colleagues cannot fully understand where the Black colleagues' pain comes from, they might dig inward and find their own pain in order to have their own pain serve as a bridge to their colleagues'. If other forms of progress follow the initial feeling of empathy, then this concept of stealing down pain is an initial step on a developmental journey.

Over time, we have heard many White students and colleagues respond to racialized pain with stories of childhood trauma and other stories of suffering. In response to stories of racism their colleagues of color share, they respond with their own stories of pain. The first time we heard a student share a painful (yet unrelated to diversity) story, we were shocked; the collective focus of our conversation quickly shifted toward addressing and empathizing with the individual and her pain that it simultaneously de-emphasized the focus of racialized pain that was initially shared. However, it turned out that each time we engaged in deep and meaningful dialogue around racism, someone invariably would steal down the pain of others, and share her or his own painful stories, of something, anything, other than racial injustice. Perhaps the vulnerable moments experienced as a group in a safe space elicits a deeper unconscious feeling of a need to share something painful for the good of the order. However, when someone shares his or her history of abuse by a family member in the context of a diversity and social justice class, we ponder the driving logic and rationale. In fact, each time a story of deep grief and anguish like molestation is shared, the conversation shifts to appropriately address that individual's emotional need and state of vulnerability. There seemed to be a collective desire to cut these people some slack. They hurt too. They clearly have experienced deep pain.

After several years, it was clear that this trend was pervasive—White students sharing their individual pain claims as a response to examples of systemic pain among students of color. Again, without knowing the intent of those who share their pain stories (perhaps they felt they had nothing else to contribute to a discussion or sought to be empathetic), the net effect is that these stories detract from the pain of lived experiences for people of color. When we witness people digging into their emotional storage and pulling out the experience of divorce in response to someone talking about a microaggression, we realize that there is a larger underlying phenomenon. In the setting of a class or a workshop, revealing an experience of family molestation may seem appropriate, but it is also an indication of downplaying or ignoring systemic racism that happens to millions of people of color over the last two hundred years. I (Collins) find the response to be deep and unconscious, but also White Out—an attempt to blot out one experience with a very heavy and emotional experience. My pain is worse than your pain. It is stealing down the pain. Your pain, I acknowledge, but mine is greater, therefore, you have no reason to be upset; this logic may be the dark underbelly of meritocracy. Although the empathy may be genuine, it may also be a proxy for conveying, "Oh you hurt? So do I. Oh, someone called you n[word]? I got robbed." So whose pain is worse? Who gets more sympathy in the classroom or another social space? In the end, stealing down the pain serves to invalidate that someone may have a legitimate pain claim related to race.

We have heard many painful stories of divorce, childhood trauma, abuse, eating disorders, and struggles with weight; we acknowledge and empathize with all the individual pain. However, we submit that these stories are not necessarily the result of a systemic or historic accumulation of generations of colonization, legal maneuvering, forced immigration through slavery, or economic disenfranchisement in the United States and around the world.

## White-Upping the Other

Swapping war stories, playing a perpetual game of White-Up, may be part of the logic that drives these types of responses to people of color. Prisoners might do this about their escapades that led them to prison. New parents might engage in this behavior among friends, talking about child rearing, their children's messy bowel movements, sleep deprivation, and what crazy thing happened on the airplane. We have seen young men one up each other as part of daily locker room banter.

So one component of White-Up and stealing down the pain is a natural inclination to tell a better story—to be competitive. White-upping is a defense mechanism where White people, uncomfortable with stories of racism from People of Color, steal pain and begin disclosing their own individual pain. This behavior can be a response that is unconscious and unintentional; still, it is important to recognize the distinctions between an individual pain, where a stratified society did not condition or predispose the experience, and the pain derived from a systemic injustice. Stealing pain defends White dominance by rejecting systemic pain claims.

I (Jun) recall a conversation I had with some graduate students several years ago. One African American female was sharing about her experiences of being a Black woman in school, and being called a variety of racially derogatory terms. She proceeded to share her story from the fifth grade about being called n[word] and people touching her hair. A White male colleague jumped in and shared that when he played basketball in high school, he was the only White player (later we learned that the school was predominantly White except for the basketball and football teams), and everybody called him White Shadow. "So, I understand where you are coming from" was his ultimate retort. He failed to recognize the systemic and perpetual nature of racism she experienced. In refusing to acknowledge her pain, he stole her pain; by disputing pain claims, he obscured the systemic nature of the experiences. This conversation serves as an example of the "I also can relate to your pain because this happened to me too" competition. Although externally claiming, "I hurt too," the intent behind his comment was not one of empathy. He did not relate to her. He was communicating that she was not the only one who has suffered.

Defensive pain claims can occur anonymously or at least at a distance through social media. A primary example of these claims occurs in places like the University of Missouri in 2015 and other sites of protest where tolerance for racial inequity is waning. As a response to ongoing racism on campus, some students went on hunger strikes and held demonstrations and rallies across the campus calling for the resignation of the university's president. The football team then decided to boycott (first the Black players and then eventually the entire team). The boycott preceded the eventual resignation of both the university's President as well as the University of Missouri system's Chancellor. The critiques of this movement and countless others like it on social media have had a consistent pattern: students today are too sensitive, too politically correct, and are being coddled.

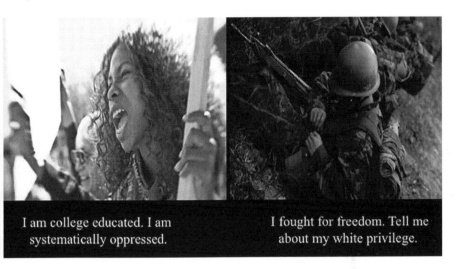

I am college educated. I am systematically oppressed.

I fought for freedom. Tell me about my white privilege.

Figure 2.1. A Replica of Wussified Whiners by Sarah Palin

Figure 2.1, is similar to a meme found on Alaska governor Sarah Palin's Facebook page, which included her comment, "YOUR BRAIN ON COLLEGE: WUSSIFIED WHINERS PROVE WHAT A WASTE IT'S BECOMING." This image and the embedded comments encapsulated the essence of pain claims through "I hurt too" as a way of shutting down the claims of others. The convenient comparison in this case is between a college student who started a hunger strike to create awareness of racial injustices, and a WWII soldier who died for his country. It is ironic that military policies at the time of the second Great War to end fascism in Europe, had a segregated units, which simply mirrored the ongoing pre-civil rights Jim Crow laws back home in the United States. The "I hurt too" mentality here encapsulates White feelings of frustration with and trivialization of the complaints of people of color.

The two variations of "I hurt too" fit directly within the overall White Out structure, which demonstrates that a person will unconsciously use a variety of tools and strategies. We underscore the importance of acknowledging that this does not make a White individual a bad person, but rather a participant in a broader system that reinforces White dominance.

## Emotional Appropriation

Stealing pain can take on different forms as well. Rachel Dolezal,[3] the former National Association for the Advancement of Colored People (NAACP) chapter in Spokane, Washington, made news in the summer of 2015 with the revelation that she is not Black, as revealed by her White parents. She grew up with four adopted Black siblings and developed a great sense of passion for the Black experience. Eventually, she went to Howard University, married a Black man, and at some point began adjusting her physical appearance (hair style and skin tone) to look Black. One response to her identity presentation was that it was a deeper level of Blackface and cultural appropriation. During the same summer, Caitlyn Jenner (formerly Bruce) had just presented herself to the world as a woman. A variety of voices criticized those who supported Jenner and not Dolezal asking why is it acceptable to change your gender and/or sex and not your racial identity. As it pertains to the notion of stealing pain, a key event in Dolezal's life is when she filed legal suit against Howard University for damages based on alleged discrimination including her race—White.[4] The transition from White and allegations for discrimination based on being White to Black is one fraught with questions about the motivation and intent. This case is pertinent to concepts in Chapter 3, but it exemplifies a complicated notion of appropriating or even stealing pain followed by a guise of sameness.

### Injustice versus Systemic Injustice

There are multiple interpretations of the word injustice. We can play games with words like justice when a colleague says, "my perpetrator never came to justice, so I know what you mean when you say you were oppressed." One obvious problem with a statement like this is that it feels like a game of Oppression Olympics. We acknowledge that an individual caused great pain. It is horrible and tragic. Recounting those memories will evoke empathy in most listeners. However, it was not systemic in the same way acts of racism, sexism, and homophobia are perpetuated at both the individual and structural level. The White architecture of the mind is individual, but the blueprints come from a system. Further internalization of those blueprints continues to perpetuate the system and find new ways to deal with attempts to invalidate the architecture (i.e., the system). Saying "I hurt too" erases the significance of systemic injustices and the systems that perpetuate them. One White person's isolated, yet painful, experience does not measure the same as the Black American experience, which represents generations of enslavement, of ancestors brought over on slave boats, laws created to prevent economic, physical, and psychological well being in the form of Jim Crow laws, redlining in real estate market, and the resultant subpar public education. An isolated violation of one person's individual right to safety is not the same as the generational consequences of genocide and land theft of Indigenous Americans, the illegal occupation of the sovereign Hawai'i, or of Japanese American internment following WWII. In the White architecture of the mind, individualistic evaluations are pervasive, which tend to avoid or White Out systemic issues where an individual is predisposed toward a certain outcome based on their social location.

As an extension of the difference between individual and systemic racism, it is important to highlight the distinction between prejudice and racism. Prejudice consists of individual assumptions and preconceived notions that are often negative and applied toward certain groups, including implicit and explicit biases. As I (Jun) and others have argued elsewhere, prejudice is different from racism in that racism is individual prejudice multiplied by power.[5] Racism is therefore systemic prejudice that involves power as a key dynamic in dominance.

## Black Lives Matter? All Lives Matter!

Following an immense amount of media coverage, the discussion of Black Lives Matter (BLM)/All Lives Matter was presented as a question in the first democratic presidential primary debate in 2015. All Lives Matter emerged as a retort to the Black Lives Matter movement. Claiming that all lives matter should carry the meaning that there is some level of equity or that everybody has the same opportunity. However, an examination of whether or not all lives matter is quickly resolved with evidence in prison rates, incarceration rates, income inequality, and educational access. Presidential candidate Bernie Sanders responded to the question about Black Lives Matter.[6]

Anderson Cooper:   From Arthur in Des Moines: Do black lives matter or do all lives matter? Let's put that question to Senator Sanders.

Bernie Sanders:    Black lives matter, and the reason those words matter is the African American community knows that on any given day, some innocent person like Sandra Bland can get into a car, and then three days later she's going to end up dead in jail or their kids are gonna get shot. We need to combat institutional racism from top to bottom, and we need major, major reforms in a broken criminal justice system in which we have more people in jail than China. I intend to tackle that issue to make sure that our people have education and jobs rather than jail cells.

Daryl Smith and other scholars on diversity have expressed the importance of remaining focused on unfinished work of centuries-long struggles against systemic oppression in the U.S.[7] Our focus on Whiteness does not serve as a disavowal that there are other issues of social justice. However, we want to orient our discussion of justice around race because of the fifty years of unfinished work. In the context of pain claims, we receive resistance—some people want to focus on something other than race, like weight, ability, or gender. We acknowledge the work of Smith, Crenshaw, and others in situating race as not the only factor, but an important one in intersectionality. The role of gender is fundamentally important, but when White women default to only gender, or even gender first, within their pain claims, it subordinates the role of race within that intersectionality and the systemic and perpetual injustices of racism. In fact, it is a very subtle yet destructive approach to derailing discussions of race, because it denies and waters down racism. Perhaps this tactic of challenging the BLM movement by saying that all lives matter is intentional. By saying Black lives matter, there is no imbedded suggestion that White lives or other lives do not matter. While efforts to explore motivation and intent are good, ultimately this discussion is about impact.

## A Way Forward

We argue in this chapter that White folks ought to become conscious of the ways they erase the pain of others through their own White pain, whether intentional or not, because the impact is the same in conversations about racial injustice. The notion of colonizing pain, while discussed here as an individual act, ought to be interrogated in greater depth from a systemic perspective. White people have been imprinted with a way of encountering race problems in the U.S. from a dominant position for so long that even without intending to do so, they extract emotional resources from those with less power.

At the same time, intersectionality as a framework for this discussion is invaluable.[8] Our intent is to recognize the multiple intersections of identity, rather than be myopic in our understanding reasons for stealing pain; intersectionality would suggest that Whites also experience systemic pain, not just individual pain. We submit that people ought to consider a third way—White folks learn the art of *holding* another's pain. Moreover, people in a dominant group need to develop strategies of holding another's pain in the same way that they hold their own pain. This is especially true as they occupy dominant space in conversations about racial injustice. White folks in dominant spaces should absolutely recognize, share, and hold onto their own pain, yet they ought to also ensure that they hold on to their own pain while simultaneously placing systemic pain of racialized "others" in the forefront. Failure to do so may unwittingly continue to defend White dominance, and continue to erase the racialized pain that people of color experience not only as individuals but also as part of an enduring systemic reality for multiple generations.

Whenever a student or colleague's contribution to a discussion on racial injustice notes a personal struggle with weight, is that person missing the point or getting the point? We submit that the student has missed the bigger systemic issue surrounding race, and the contribution of a personal struggle with weight Whited out the point. Weight is an important issue, no doubt. Although there is prejudice against people with various shapes and sizes, it does not have the same historical precedence, significance, and cumulative effect that people are still experiencing today. Gentrification does not happen when skinny people invade neighborhoods. You cannot disaggregate prison populations and analyze criminal behavior by people who were bullied. You cannot look at income inequality simply by people with divorced parents. However, some communities have higher rates of type 2 juvenile diabetes because of a lack of healthy food options in urban communities and an overabundance of processed food that is convenient and cheap—not because of nutritional habits and diet. The root of the inequity is in race, not the byproduct of weight, size, and health.

We are focusing on a specific phenomenon that occurs within the White architecture of the mind that ultimately defends White dominance. Whenever the focus shifts the discussion away from race to weight, poverty, divorce, or even childhood trauma, it assuages the guilt and pain of confronting systemic racism. Considering every possible source of individual pain obscures systemic consequences of racial injustice. It colonizes pain. It steals pain.

Lastly, there is an ongoing debate about whether or not White guilt is useful in discussions of race and diversity. Guilt is another layer of pain. Some contend that White guilt is fundamentally not useful because the hyper individualistic focus prevents people from seeing the larger system at work. Others find that if guilt is the starting point for a developmental journey that leads to greater levels of consciousness, then it can be useful. Brené Brown highlighted the difference between guilt and shame.[9] Brown generally defined guilt as a failure that can be assessed against an individual's set of values and standards. Discomfort can be used for growth. Shame, however, is the feeling of being deeply flawed or unworthy. Whenever we say the word White in the context of a diversity seminar or workshop, it can change the environment in the room. People become uncomfortable and we believe it is related to feelings of shame in the absence of guilt. Participants wonder why they feel so bad even though they do not feel they have done anything wrong. We advocate that shame should be concretely associated with White systems and that individuals should assess their guilt in ways that create consciousness around systemic impact regardless of the intent. White pain claims should be suspended when listening to accounts of racial injustice, even if the initial instinct is to try and share something similar. Listening, lamenting, and grieving are communal ways of *hearing* pain instead of making claims and *stealing* pain.

## Notes

1.  Memmi, Albert. *The colonizer and the colonized*. New York: Routledge, 2013.
2.  Several scholars of Critical Race Theory have been instrumental in driving new research on understanding race and racism in the United States. Read the work of Delgado, Richard, and Jean Stefancic. *Critical race theory: The cutting edge*. Philadelphia: Temple University Press, 2000.
    Read also the work of Gloria Ladson Billings and her colleague William Tate. Ladson-Billings, Gloria, and William F. Tate. "Toward a critical race theory of education." *Teachers College Record* 97, no. 1 (1995): 47.
3.  Richard, Perez-Pena. "Rachel Dolezal leaves N.A.A.C.P. post as past discrimination suit is revealed," *New York Times*, last modified June 12, 2015, http://nyti.ms/1MF2ytM
4.  Ibid.
5.  Jun, Alexander, "Unintentional racism," in *Heal us, Emmanuel: A call for racial reconciliation, representation, and unity in the church*, ed. Doug Serven (Oklahoma City: Black White Bird Press, 2016), 21–26.

6. "Bernie Sanders: Black lives matter," *CNN Politics*, last modified October 13, 2015, http://www.cnn.com/videos/politics/2015/10/13/bernie-sanders-democratic-debate-black-lives-matter-27.cnn

7. Smith, Daryl G. *Diversity's promise for higher education: Making it work*. Baltimore: JHU Press, 2015.

8. Crenshaw, Kimberlé. *Critical race theory: The key writings that formed the movement*. New York: The New Press, 1995.

9. Brown, Brené. *Daring greatly: How the courage to be vulnerable transforms the way we live, love, parent, and lead*. New York: Penguin Books, 2012.

# Chapter Three

# Whitefluenza: How Privilege Is an Epidemic with No Known Cure

## Introduction and Epidemiology

We have spent some time in emergency rooms and have taken days off of work to see a primary care doctor for our sick children. Fever, vomiting, chills, aches and pain. With hopeful anticipation we have looked to our ER doctors and pediatricians to tell us that their illness is bacterial—that it can be treated with antibiotics. Oftentimes, the doctors respond with the dreaded news: it is a virus. No known medicine can effectively treat a virus. A virus is hard to treat—it lives in the cells of our bodies and is essentially protected from medicine. The unique, protected, and complex nature of viruses make it an apt metaphor for White privilege. For example, White privilege is like a virus that evolves, mutates, and rapidly spreads; it is very difficult to prevent or defeat. This analogy provides many levels of analysis for understanding how White privilege reproduces and spreads through the architecture of the White mind and through dominant White systems and culture.

A common virus like the flu may be painful for a short time, but it eventually passes. A more serious virus like the human immunodeficiency virus (HIV) never goes away. Other viruses can lay dormant for a decade or more with symptoms emerging only occasionally. All components of the individual effects of viruses provide useful analogies for exploring how privilege manifests in acute and isolated cases. For White folks at various stages of consciousness, privilege may be visible and leveraged on a daily basis; for others, the manifestations appear to be acute and temporary and then eventually pass. However, even when individual symptoms dissipate, the virus is still alive, spreading, and mutating. As a virus replicates over time, the genes of the virus continually make small changes. As changes are made, human bodies do not recognize the viruses. These changes and genetic drifts are why people continue to be infected by viruses even as their bodies continues to build immunities. As a result, the individual effects of White privilege provide a narrow and truncated way of understanding privilege. Whitefluenza is the notion that White privilege spreads, mutates, lies dormant, is more visible at various times due to acute symptoms, and is part of a larger system where members unwittingly change the rules or perspectives to maintain dominance. At times, there may be outbreaks and even epidemics; other times, there are inoculations. During both scenarios, the systemic culture of the virus is alive and well. Similar to how the norovirus can ravage families, schools, and communities, Whitefluenza spreads through the mind of individuals and societies. It is embedded in the White architecture of the mind.

The virus spreads through the ways people speak, think, act, respond, retaliate, educate, and engage. For example, I (Collins) grew up hearing racist language *outside* of my home. I have family in Alabama and I grew up in Tennessee, Louisiana, Kansas, and Texas, where overt discrimination was common. This overt model of racism represents one strand of the virus that I knew I didn't have. But, because I grew up seeing and hearing this type of racism outside of my home, I dealt with another strand of the virus that was harder for me to detect. Having the ability to point to something that I clearly was not (an overt bigot) veiled my ability to see narrower and microaggressive strands of privilege and bias in action. These weaker strands of the virus are a key defender in maintaining White dominance. Inability to see the virus supports its survival and prevents inoculation in the form of recognition and consciousness. Societies represent constructed realities where any advantage is clung to and fought for with a great sense of entitlement. Examples like generational wealth, entitlements, and trickle up economics (the rich are getting richer and the poor are getting poorer) are all indications of how a belief in ownership creates a sense of protectionism. Feelings of entitlement lead to astounding resilience and dedication toward defending dominance.

## Endowed Privilege

When people own material goods they tend to overestimate its value because they are in possession, whether it is a small memento or something much larger (e.g., a house). This pattern—where people demand much more to give up an object than they would be willing to pay to acquire it—is called the *endowment effect*[1] or *status quo bias*.[2] A more complex example of this idea is something called a virtual endowment, which refers to the feeling of ownership people feel even before something is owned, which goes beyond just physical ownership to include attitudes, behaviors, and viewpoints. Once people experience ownership toward an idea, it is difficult to let the idea go, which results in a rigid and unyielding ideology.[3] Cultures with systemic privilege and instant gratification draw blue prints and schemas within the mind about entitlements and rights. Privilege is in an architecturally safe house within the White architecture of the mind. It is, however, not immutable.

Endowment effects are a manifestation of an asymmetry of value. This *loss aversion* occurs when the disutility of giving up an object is greater than the utility associated with acquiring it. This phenomenon occurs as individuals focus on what they may lose, rather than what they may gain. Whenever there is uncertainty, the losses appear larger than the potential gains.[4] In a traditionally rational sense, having any kind of privilege creates a sense of endowment and it is irrational to consider doing anything to jeopardize or even compromise that valuable asset. As a result, privilege grows and is transferred with a sense of rationality that gives it virus-like qualities.

Again, when going to the doctor for a fever and congestion, patients hope they have a bacterial infection and the doctor will write a prescription for antibiotics. However, if they have a viral infection, they will have to wait for their body to suppress the active infection instead of finding a solution. A virus is a microscopic infectious agent that replicates and mutates inside of other living organisms. A virus can spread in many different ways and survive as very small particles when not infecting a host. A healthy immune system can eliminate some viruses and vaccines can inoculate a host from being infected. Privilege acts in many of the same ways by promoting and protecting dominant Whiteness; it often operates more effectively when undetected or acknowledged. As a result, White privilege can thrive if perceived as dormant or only when producing a low-grade fever. Subtle manifestations of White privilege serve to maintain White dominance in a multicultural age. As overt outbreaks draw more attention and more action directed at the root of the problem, the evolving virus maintains position when paired with unconsciousness.

Some obvious and overt instances of White privilege in the racial history of the US include the ability to own people of a different race, defining people of a different race as less than a full person, and preventing them from participating fully in civic affairs, in addition to many other examples. These privileges and their effects were so overt that even though people fought desperately to keep them, they could not survive the test of a populous history and the emergence of a multicultural age. As a result, overt racism was traded in for something much easier to hide. The initiation of Civil Rights and full participation for minorities in government affairs produced the ability to argue that everyone has the same opportunity. For example, arguments that any inequality in outcomes was rooted in personal moral failings emerged. At this point, White privilege became much more like a virus—it was more difficult to see, but the effects were insidious.

## Admit Your White Privilege

In order to examine deeper layers of Whitefluenza, we turn to an interesting and televised exchange between two popular media personalities. Jon Stewart, the liberal former host of The Daily Show, convinced the conservative Fox News commentator Bill O'Reilly to appear on his show in October 2014 to promote a book. Within the first moments of the conversation, Stewart said, "I have one simple goal. I want you to admit that there is such a thing as White privilege. That's all I want from you today."[5] The segment was entertaining to watch and one that is easy to find via the Internet. O'Reilly responded, "In your case, there is White privilege," but clarified that he did not actually believe that there is a thing called White privilege, and if there is, there has to be Asian privilege, "because Asians make more money than Whites." From that point, Stewart struggled to translate his learned, book knowledge of the differences and nuances of White privilege into quick, made-for-TV banter:

> So it's really—they're not equivalent. And either way, White people, males, set the system so that's what privilege is—is that White people set the system that, yes, maybe Asian immigrants want immigration policy liberalized, have done better over these past 30 or 40 years. But there has been a systemic— systemic systematized subjugation of the Black community.

If you find Stewart's words hard to read, it was also difficult to listen to. He was not communicating well. It was clear he believed something different than O'Reilly, but was not able to clarify what it was. The debate moved on from the poorly explained Asian American perspective and focused on the difference between the past and the present, as O'Reilly noted: "Maybe you haven't figured out that there is no more slavery, no more Jim Crow, all right, and the most powerful man in the world is—a Black American."

Stewart became more frustrated at this point and struggled to explain to O'Reilly the residual impact of "systemic subjugation." O'Reilly conceded that collectively some of this may be true, but that ultimately people still have individual choice. He told Stewart, "Listen, this is the usual White guilt liberal stuff that you guys throw out there forever." From there, Stewart probably made the most poignant argument in this bumpy discussion. He drew O'Reilly into acknowledging how geography, neighborhoods, and upbringing leave an imprint on lives, including O'Reilly's own upbringing in Levittown, NY where his father was able to purchase a home with an affordable mortgage via the GI Bill in the 1950s. The crux of the conversation occurred when O'Reilly acknowledged that Black people could not live in his neighborhood at the time. The connection put pressure on his logic and he reverted back to saying it is not *that* nice of a place to live, but added, "Alright. If you want to say it's White privilege because Whites didn't have it as bad as blacks, fine." O'Reilly added several other platitudes about hard work, any one can make it, and the accusation that Stewart was ultimately pushing "victimhood."

Stewart worked diligently to convince or convert O'Reilly's conservative disposition. The exchange, however, provided additional layers with which to understand the concept of Whitefluenza. O'Reilly's response shows more *overt* layers of privilege and denial. For some who already accept the notion of White privilege, the conservative disposition will come across as unconsciousness. Stewart's point about the systems built into geography and neighborhoods is poignant. However, the larger point about the mutating role of the virus is less about O'Reilly's disposition and more about Stewart's. Whitefluenza is perhaps more vibrant in persons who believe they have a deep understanding of diversity in a multicultural age. Stewart is a good example.

Following Stewart's show, there were plenty of accolades for Stewart and his gotcha moment about O'Reilly and his childhood home. There were also criticisms. When O'Reilly was leaning on aggregated pan-Asian American incomes in comparison to White incomes as proof of no White privilege unless there was Asian privilege, Stewart awkwardly tried to counter and asked, "What kind of Asians?" The author of the blog Reappropriate, noted,

> In a world where Asian Americans make up less than 3% of those appearing even as guests on political talk shows, it's not entirely surprising that there

was no Asian American (or indeed no person of color at all) to help salvage this travesty of a Whitesplaining moment.[6]

The article included a breakdown of the size of Asian American households, income contributors, and prevalence in expensive areas, which mitigate the static and linear comparison of incomes. The issue is much deeper. Privilege is not measured by income. There are nuanced factors that contribute to a system of privilege, and history is an important predictor of the future (the article noted that Levittown, NY is still 95 percent White today). In the end, there were no people of color on the segment. It was two White men—one struggling to articulate a position on diversity, privilege, and racial minorities, and the other denying that any concrete difference exists.

Stewart's role in this discussion becomes more interesting in this brief case study of Whitefluenza because of incidents of working with writers of color. For example, a 2015 New York Times article included an account of a dispute on the Daily Show about a racially insensitive segment.[7] A former writer on Stewart's show disclosed a heated exchange about a segment that he perceived as racially insensitive (a portrayal of a conservative Black politician). He outlined how Stewart became insensitive and shouted expletives regarding the disagreement. The writer, who is Black, summarized how Stewart impersonating a Black politician was "a little weird" and discouraged any repetition of the segment. Stewart shut him down—repeatedly. The argument grew in intensity and volume as the two men crossed the building to Stewart's office. Later, Stewart apologized to the staff, but the only Black writer on the show felt disrespected. When the exchange was detailed in a podcast, Stewart reached out to the writer and "kind of apologized" for if the writer "felt hurt." Stewart is liberal and engages in discussions of race, diversity, equity, and other issues of dominance. He is considered to be someone who understands the issues and used his platform to educate, inform, and advocate. However, he demonstrated inconsistencies and manifestations of Whitefluenza that are not unique and raise a different challenge for White allies, which we discuss in greater detail in a chapter entitled, White 22.

In my (Collins) own racial identity development, I have often coveted the *Black pat*—that is the pat on the back from a Black person confirming my status as an ally, someone who has a greater understanding of the issues. The desire for such confirmation as a badge of honor confirms another characteristic of White privilege as a virus. It represents yet another space (social and geographic) where I can walk without fear, garner respect, and validate my status and identity. Becoming an ally adds to a privileged endowment. There is so much denial of White privilege at face value that allies who admit White privilege often fall in the trap of using acknowledgement as a way to gain privilege instead of continuously interrogating the role of White privilege in their interior and exterior life. The shifting nature of examined and unexamined privilege is a symptom of Whitefluenza. The role of endowment in Whitefluenza becomes clear when you try to remove the badge or the Black pat from the liberal White ally. Removing a badge that validates the role of a White liberal incites anger, rage, disappointment, resentment, accusations of ungrateful recipients, and unveils another side privilege. This scenario was the case in the Stewart vignette, and in my own experience on a journey seeking validation as a White ally.

Experiences that lead to (or perhaps shield) the badge represented by the Black pat include, but are not limited to, having a friend of color (or two), not using the n[word], disparaging racial prejudice when sitting with a friend of color, taking a diversity class in college, attending a Black church (once), living in another country as a voluntary minority, or even adopting a child who is not White. Many of these experiences are voluntary and are accompanied by the ability to return to dominantly White spaces, including friend groups, churches, universities, neighborhoods, and country clubs. When challenged again about privilege, these experiences are readily available to assuage guilt or to renew credentials leading to the Black pat. Even when White allies are under threat of losing the privilege associated with being an ally, the privilege must evolve.

## Shedding Whiteness

Rachel Dolezal is a case of Whitefluenza evolution gone extreme and awry. Born with all of the characteristics of being White, including White parents, a White community, and a White identity, Dolezal eventually grew to claim an African American identity as an adult. Her story is lengthy and continuously unfolding, but some of the key elements of her case begin with the fact that her parents are White and she has adopted brothers who are Black. Her White parents maintained that she is White and her adopted Black brothers identified that she is White. One of her brothers compared her racial identity evolution to Blackface.[8] Her claims were complicated as she avoided direct questions, claimed she did not understand questions about her race, and indicated that everyone was from the African continent. She has Black brothers, had a Black husband, has Black children, served as leader of the Spokane NAACP, and even attended a graduate program at Howard University, a historically Black institution.

The complexity of the Dolezal case emerged during her time at Howard when she sued the University for discrimination. The Court of Appeals decision noted that she claimed discrimination based on "race" and that the University favored "African American students" over her.[9] Several psychologists who study race were quoted in news outlets as saying that this is a case of over identification with a marginalized group and ultimately an archetype of White guilt pushed to the extreme.[10] As the story unfolded, she gained some clarity in her descriptions by admitting that she was born White but that she identifies as Black. Around the same time, former Olympic athlete and reality star Bruce Jenner came out as transitioning gender and identified as a woman now known as Caitlyn Jenner. Some commentators compared being transgender to being transracial and questioned why claiming a transracial identity was cultural appropriation. Although this point is complicated, it is a logical fallacy to suggest that acceptance of a transgender identity requires acceptance of a transracial decision. Many writers deal this with at length, and we advocate that race and gender are separate and that the argument for acceptance or denial of one does not dictate the other.

Using the concept of Whitefluenza, we contend that the Dolezal case is not limited to over identification, and is ultimately something much deeper than White guilt. Rachel Dolezal's racial evolution is a choice and a symptom of an evolving White privilege. The movement from suing Howard University for discrimination against being White to serving as an NAACP leader in Spokane with a Black identity is a variation in strategies that highlight a desperation for privilege in diverse and multicultural spaces. It is pathological. The mutating privilege is an unconscious participant among strategies to maintain White dominance.

## Confronting Disease

Every metaphor breaks down at some point and in order to supplement the notion of privilege as a virus, we also think of it more broadly as a disease. Alcoholism is recognized as life long abnormal condition that is broadly categorized as a disease—even when there are no acute physical manifestations of symptoms. In a traditional recovery program, there are twelve steps: the first step is, "We admitted we were powerless over alcohol—that our lives had become unmanageable." Again, no analogy is perfectly symmetrical, but for our purposes the acknowledgement of the predisposition toward alcohol is not to surrender to the fight, but to commit to a continuous diligence. This apt analogy demonstrates how the structure of the mind shapes daily thought processes. Counselors use the acronym SUDS to remind clients of *seemingly unimportant decisions*. Even for alcoholics who have been sober for 30 years with no acute systems, they may still have a mental consciousness that is predisposed for opening a mental door toward alcohol. The White architecture of the mind has been shaped by a larger White system and individuals are compelled to participate—even when unintentional and unconscious.

The decision to be conscious around issues of race and identity should address SUDS as they relate to macro and micro aggressions rooted in socially constructed categories and norms around race, gender, and other forms of identity. The acute manifestations will vary among individuals. Colleges and universities continue to be active sites of contention around race and diversity. Returning to rhetoric generated from Fox News, Bill O'Reilly had two guests on his show to talk about "campus madness," because the University of Vermont had a three day retreat on White privilege and another university brought in counselors to assist students after a confederate flag incident.[11] Mr. O'Reilly asked one of the guests if they had confronted their White privilege and they mockingly responded, "You didn't issue me a trigger warning before you asked me about my whiteness" and then claimed to have never cashed in on White privilege. Another guest on the show noted,

> The administrators and the professors are wondering how this happened on college campuses because they're eating their own. But the professors and the administrators have created this monster through their diversity programs, through their tolerance programs which really only allowed so much tolerance and tolerate nothing at all.

The title of that segment was, "White Privilege has Infected US Elite Universities." Privilege is indeed an infection, but in this particular instance it manifests as a mockery. This mockery highlights a deep disdain for even conversing about White privilege and rejects the notion that privilege and power combine as key elements of racism. Denying the existence of a virus is a crucial component of defending its ability to spread and go undetected.

Higher education is a place where transformation takes place through both retreats and protests. The continued exploration of the virus will likely weaken its ability to manifest in negative ways. However, the active involvement of White allies in movements for justice and equity can fall prey to the paradox of when helping hurts. The involvement of White individuals does not change a White system, but can be a new manifestation of privilege that advances White dominance. Addressing the virus, the disease of privilege is one way individuals can begin to acknowledge and approach the dominant system. In the end, it is not about guilt or whether or not someone is a bad person. The challenge is to find and dismantle unconscious or unintentional strategies that defend White dominance.

# Notes

1. Samuelson, William, and Richard Zeckhauser. "Status quo bias in decision making." *Journal of Risk and Uncertainty* 1, no. 1 (1988): 7–59.
2. Thaler, Richard. "Toward a positive theory of consumer choice." *Journal of Economic Behavior & Organization* 1, no. 1 (1980): 39–60.
3. Schwartz, Hugh. "Predictably Irrational: the hidden forces that shape our decisions." *Business Economics* 43, no. 4 (2008): 69–72.
4. Kahneman, Daniel, and Amos Tversky. "Choices, values, and frames."*American Psychologist* 39, no. 4 (1984): 341.
5. Taibi, Catherine, "Jon Stewart tries to make Bill O'Reilly admit white privilege exists. And fails," *Huffington Post*, last modified October 16, 2014, http://www.huffingtonpost.com/2014/10/16/jon-stewart-bill-oreilly-white-privilege-daily-show_n_5995726.html
6. "How both Bill O'Reilly and Jon Stewart got it really wrong on Asian Americans," *Reappropriate*, last modified October 16, 2014, http://reappropriate.co/2014/10/how-both-bill-oreilly-and-jon-stewart-got-it-really-wrong-on-asian-privilege/
7. Itzkoff, Dave, "Daily Show' writer recalls heated dispute with Jon Stewart," *New York Times*, last modified July 24, 2015, http://www.nytimes.com/2015/07/25/arts/television/daily-show-writer-recalls-heated-dispute-with-jon-stewart.html
8. Moyer, Justin, "'Are you an African American?' Why an NAACP official isn't saying." *The Washington Post*, last modified June 12, 2015, https://www.washingtonpost.com/news/morning-mix/wp/2015/06/12/spokane-naacp-president-rachel-dolezal-may-be-white/
9. "NAACP imposter sued school over race claims," *The Smoking Gun*, last modified June 15, 2015, http://www.thesmokinggun.com/documents/bizarre/rachel-dolezal-discrimination-lawsuit-786451
10. Thompson, Krissah, "Rachel Dolezal: What the rights activist's story says about being white in modern America," *Independent*, last modified June 15, 2015, http://www.independent.co.uk/news/world/americas/rachel-dolezal-what-the-rights-activists-story-says-about-being-white-in-modern-america-10318082.html
11. This segment of the O'Reilly Factor aired on the *Fox News* network on December 1, 2015.

# Chapter Four

# White 22: White If You Do, White If You Don't

During the 2014 wake of Michael Brown's death in Ferguson, MO, individuals and groups of people gathered to protest the shooting of another unarmed Black man. Religious groups got involved, grassroots activism emerged, and the scene of protest persisted as the decision on whether or not to indict the officer continued to drag out. We heard of a progressive White woman who felt compelled to travel to Ferguson to join the protest and be in solidarity. She wanted to join her Black brothers and sisters because of her concern for racial justice. To her dismay, rather than receiving the coveted pat on the back for showing up and for being a good White person, she was challenged by several Black protesters as to her presence. They challenged her motivation as she was yelling and screaming and attempting to link arms. They asked her, "What are you doing here?" It came as a surprise to the woman and became a real predicament in terms of trying to figure out what to do next. She spent time and money to travel across the country. She made her way to an intensely emotional scene—the heart of a struggle for justice, and was immediately challenged. Perhaps some White readers can relate to being shut down by colleagues and friends of color in moments of misunderstood solidarity. Undoubtedly there are other examples at similar rallies and protests across the nation. This chapter covers the contradictions in White activism when someone else's struggle becomes the privilege of someone who can choose to opt in to the movement.

The same kind of reflection and sentiment was offered through multiple outlets in both formal and social media. One blog was entitled, "Dear White People: Ferguson Protests are a Wake Not a Pep Rally," and included poignant reflections about the pain of feeling ontologically isolated and denied through the national events and media coverage. The author recalled attending protests and noted,

> ... white "allies" come out to support the cause, yet struggle to feel comfortable surrounded by Black people and so clump with their friends, take pictures to prove that they were there and subtly and unconsciously fight to control the space with their chants. Often, this fight for control is more obvious, like white people taking the mic and talking about why they are there....[1]

The author acknowledged that the problem is subtle, but as tragedies become momentary opportunities and moments become movements, the subtle problems are magnified. In contrast to the behavior of White allies, the author included that

> ... For many Black people, Ferguson protest [sic] are not a public pep rally for racial unity, they are a living wake. We are dying. We are being killed by the police. We are getting lynched by the media. Our souls are nearly suffocating by the pressure of being a problem.[2]

So the question remains, what is the role for White people in these spaces and movements? What constitutes suitable behavior and consciousness?

When it comes to being White in diverse spaces, a no-win or Catch 22 (in reference to Joseph Heller's bestselling book) attitude has evolved. There is a tension between the notion that inaction is an injustice and a threat to justice, and the sentiment "this is not my struggle so I won't get involved."

## Straight White Male

A play was developed depicting a character to represent the straight White male.[3] The playwright had a position in residence at Brown University where community members from various identity groups provided input for the White character they wanted to see in the performance. The sentiments were summarized by the desire for a character that would sit down, shut up, and listen. Upon the formation and presentation of the character, the same audience who helped develop the play in fact hated the character when it appeared in the performance. The passive nature of the character did not appeal to the very people who wanted to see those characteristics in motion.

At the beginning of the play the family at the center of the play is gathered around a board game that adapted Monopoly into a new called "Privilege." It is a White and liberal family and one brother pulled what is called an "excuse card." The other brother reads the card dryly: "What I just said wasn't racist/sexist/homophobic because I was joking ... Pay $50 to an LGBT organization."[4] The playwright Young Jean Lee called the task of writing the character an existential dilemma. This dilemma is a White 22—the feeling of futility that White people feel when they are criticized or challenged while engaged in racial justice.

Any individual caught in what they perceive as a no-win situation will be frustrated. White 22 carries with it some natural elements of frustration. I (Collins) found myself frustrated at times during my own White racial identity development. A fundamental dilemma occurs when someone with White privilege has a moment of clarity and tries to break through the privilege to advocate for justice and is later rejected or criticized. The previous vignette about the Ferguson protest is akin to this example. The refrain that sometimes emerges at this moment is, "I tried to help you all." Embedded in this sentiment is a root problem often called the White knight or White savior syndrome. This feels like White 22, but ultimately the assumed ownership of helpful expertise or energy can be very paternalistic and recreate problems. Critical Race Theorists criticize White involvement using the term *interest convergence* to identify that White folks get involved when there is some reciprocal benefit—this can either be the feeling of doing something savior-like or gaining access to another social setting where they are deemed acceptable.[5]

## When the Desire to Help Hurts

A book focused on poverty reduction is entitled *When Helping Hurts*, which is the concept that efforts from religiously affiliated missions organizations to help low-income communities unintentionally hurt these very communities. Efforts to help often come with a subtle and unconscious messianic air of superiority as the economically rich who are helping, which evolved through a fundamental belief in their own hard work.[6] The premise of the book is that flawed poverty alleviation design exacerbates the poverty of being in wealthy senses of superiority as well as economic poverty for the poor, accompanied with inferiority and shame. Similarly, when White folks attempt to deal with privilege and get involved diversity and justice work, the attempt to help can hurt and exacerbate the issue. It feels like a White 22. Claims of compassion fatigue, of trying but not being accepted, feeling paralyzed, and saying "it doesn't matter what I do" are all ways in which White 22 actually becomes another strategy for maintaining White dominance. The notion of attempting to help, being rejected, feeling trapped, and avoiding the internal and conscious-raising work required helps to support a deeply rooted dominant White system. Approaching diversity work with good intentions can clearly lead to a *when helping hurts* phenomenon.

Moreover, the very notion of a helping hurts critique will lead some White people to feel frustrated and want to give up. Robin Di Angelo writes about what she terms White Fragility, and it is a corollary construct that helps inform White 22 and vice versa. According to a Di Angelo,

> On the rare occasion that our worldviews, positions or entitlement are questioned, it throws us so off balance that we basically lose our minds. We become outraged, hurt, offended and so on, and push back with a range of defensive moves (cry, argue, withdraw, refuse to engage). These moves function to end the challenge and get us back on our racial footing. I term these moves white fragility.[7]

The notion of when helping hurts extends further into the psychology of alleviating a global problem like poverty. The notion extends into the development industry that has accompanied the construction of global inequality. Development discourse supports the idea that Africa and the southern hemisphere need Northern and Western interventions.[8] It centers the White north in relation to the needs of others who have been Othered by middle-class White northern knowledge systems and values. Heron's book, *Desire for Development*, provides a theoretical building block through recognizing that White bourgeois identity formation includes thinking of her/himself as a moral agent. The book excavates of the notion of desire and the longing for Whiteness, which carries the promise of wholeness. Looking at systemic Whiteness on this global scale where Canadian women (in the case of Heron's book) exhibit a strong desire to help, unveils the elongated driving desire to be in the right, ok, innocent, and without blame. White guilt plays a role in this phenomenon as well. Wherever guilt exists it must be alleviated. To be White is to be all right, and if there is evidence of wrongdoing then White innocence is in question. As a result the desire for development, or in our case, the desire for diversity is again about the moral compass for the maintained dominance of the White system. Claiming that an attempt was made and it is a no-win situation supports the current system and becomes a barrier to deeper layers of consciousness.

Given the intersectionalities of identity for White women, it is interesting to note how White women intentionally and unintentionally hinder the progress of racial justice. While the role and impact of some White women in the movement toward gender equality is clear, their role in diversity can get complicated sometimes—and may not be addressed in literature often. Frances Kendell's book on privilege has an excellent chapter on this issue of how White women perpetuate white supremacy.[9] In chapter eight (Good White Friends) we discuss what it means to be an effective ally as opposed to a barrier to people of color advancing and thriving in their various spheres of work and life.

Similar to Heron's and Kendall's excavation of White women, Patton and Bondi conducted a study on White men who were perceived to be in support of diversity and equity movements in higher education and entitled it, *Nice White Men or Social Justice Allies,* and the primary issue was, how do these men construct this role and navigate the complexities?[10] Central to the background of the study was the primary understanding of an ally as someone who is working towards justice from a dominant position (e.g. a straight person in support of gay and lesbian people). Dominant group membership is a prerequisite for being an ally, and in the case of White allies, one author noted, "The desire to be and be known as a good white person stems from the recognition that our whiteness is problematic, a recognition that we try to escape by being demonstrably different from other, racist whites."[11] Patton and Bondi argued that White men have the most to lose in the pursuit of social justice. This may be true in some instances, but they also have something to profit by gaining the ability to navigate a new social space (see Whitefluenza and the early quote, "The very acknowledgement of our racism and privilege can be turned to our advantage")[12]. They also make the point that some White men have experienced oppression related to socioeconomic status or being gay, but that their whiteness and maleness affords them more ability to negotiate and surpass the obstacles. Participants in the study worked to *help* individuals in difficult situations, remove systemic barriers like standardized test scores, and other actions that they found to be personally meaningful. Ultimately the authors of the study found that the participants were engaged more in *nice guy* activities that ultimately did not challenge the core of the system. The authors encouraged people who identify with the participants to continue wrestling with the question, "What right do I have to do this work," and to think about it institutionally and systemically, not just individually. For those still focused on individuality and seeking personal fulfillment in racial justice, we submit the South African concept of *unbuntu,* which is loosely translated as human-ness (I am not fully human until you are fully human).

The notion of being stuck or paralyzed is also part of a widespread notion of White racial identity development, which was articulated by Helms.[13] Part of the development is overcoming racist attitudes or behaviors, which are assumed to exist in everyone. There is a well developed body of literature that is built upon the belief that White persons should move through stages of identity development that move from ignorance and colorblindness to an increasing recognition of Whiteness and working through guilt to becoming an autonomous and racially aware being. One study argued that most university campuses are safe and comfortable White spaces that actually foster racial-arrested development, which serves to continue to reproduce existing hierarchies.[14] Our point is also that stagnation supports White dominance. Disrupting the stagnation that supports White dominance is both important and difficult. We offer a more thorough discussion of some literature and findings from our own research in chapter eight, Good White Friends.

When trying to dislodge the paralysis of White 22, a return to the fortified safety of pain claims is typical (refer back to chapter two, White Pain). This makes intergroup dialogues difficult because White people (most notably university students) begin claiming the same disenfranchised status as students of color and other marginalized groups. It is ironic to hear a White participant criticize victimhood and feign to claim victim status in a moment of White theatricality. Cabrera and other authors advocated that in order to prevent White racial arrested development, intergroup dialogues must facilitate and embrace discomfort.[15] Individual discomfort should also point to systemic questions so that issues of race are not seen as completely personal. The notion of feeling caught in a White 22 is akin to White racial arrested development.

## When to Sit Down—The Speech Heard 'Round the Internet

In June 2016, the multiracial actor, Jesse Williams, accepted the humanitarian award from BET (Black Entertainment Television). His acceptance speech was an instantaneously viral and invigorating challenge. It is worth quoting at length here:

> There has been no war that we have not fought and died on the front lines of. There has been no job we haven't done. There is no tax they haven't levied against us—and we've paid all of them. But freedom is somehow always conditional here. "You're free," they keep telling us ... Now, freedom is always

coming in the hereafter, but you know what, though, the hereafter is a hustle. We want it now. And let's get a couple things straight, just a little side note— the burden of the brutalized is not to comfort the bystander. That's not our job, alright—stop with all that. If you have a critique for the resistance, for our resistance, then you better have an established record of critique of our oppression. If you have no interest, if you have no interest in equal rights for black people then do not make suggestions to those who do. Sit down.

We've been floating this country on credit for centuries, yo, and we're done watching and waiting while this invention called whiteness uses and abuses us, burying black people out of sight and out of mind while extracting our culture, our dollars, our entertainment like oil—black gold, ghettoizing and demeaning our creations then stealing them, gentrifying our genius and then trying us on like costumes before discarding our bodies like rinds of strange fruit. The thing is though … the thing is that just because we're magic doesn't mean we're not real.[16]

The video of the acceptance speech was covered by every major news outlet and went viral on social media. The response to the acceptance speech was divided. On one side many people felt he articulated critical points from a valuable platform. On the other side are White responses that represent the concept of White 22. Justin Timberlake was one of millions of viewers watching and inspired by the speech and tweeted that he was inspired. Another Twitter user responded, "So does this mean you're going to stop appropriating our music and culture?" to which Timberlake replied, "Oh, you sweet soul. The more you realize that we are the same, the more we can have a conversation. Bye." The response ignited a plethora of comments to Timberlake including photos of him in cornrows, wave caps, and other images used to indicate his appropriation of Black culture. Three hours after the original post and the hundreds of comments that followed, Timberlake tweeted that he felt "misunderstood" and "I really do feel that we are all one … A human race."[17]

The Williams speech was a moment of clarity and even revelry as BET attendees stood before the speech was over and postings multiplied at a rapid pace. Timberlake's involvement and eventual apologizing to "anyone that felt I was out of turn" shifted the focus back to the complexity of White association and involvement, which manifests in appropriation. The lackluster apology pushed the White 22 moment through cycles of colorblindness, rejection, and White guilt.

Conservative commentator Tomi Lahren delivered a more overt articulation of resistance to the acceptance speech. Embedded in her critique were a few highlights of what have become classically White responses to revolutionary thought. Lahren said:

> Well the BET awards were last night, notably they were very Black. Oh! But can I say that, what with my *Whiteness* and all? Well too damn bad! Question— Was this a celebration of Black entertainment or an opportunity to complain about the plight of wealthy Black actors and musicians? Curious, because I saw a lot of talent on that stage but at the same time, a whole lot of victim-hood. Oh, and police bashing, that too ...
>
> Equal Rights? Please tell me Mr. Williams what rights Black people don't have? Also, White people? We do, in fact, have a record of critique of your oppression! In fact, do you know how many of our ancestors fought in the Civil War to free your ancestors? Bloodiest war in the United States history was over what was right and it was largely White people fighting in it. In fact it was White Southern Democrats who fought for, not against slavery.... I'm sorry Jesse but I won't be apologizing for my Whiteness, just as you don't need to apologize for your Blackness! It's not White people working to divide America! It's you![18]

Several popular media personalities make a living by designing overt responses to viral events or messages. In this case, Lahren's rhetoric taps into the notion of (a) boundaries about what White people can or cannot say, (b) Black people who are wealthy, which is presumed to undercut any message or claims about systemic racism, (c) protesting police violence equated with unfairly attacking the police, (d) the role of White people in the Civil War as the hero, and (e) that people of color are a problem because they keep talking about diversity.

If Williams' message had not been so widely distributed through social media and other outlets, it would never have garnered the attention of commentators. The message censured the naysayers who advocate that there is nothing race-based about the division of benefits in the US. The bimodal White response was a weak and shallow message of solidarity on one side and complete rejection and mockery on the other side. In the end, both responses are stuck in a mire of White 22—you are White if you agree and White if you do not. Williams' metaphor that those who critique resistance without critiquing oppression should "sit down" also reflects the difficulty in writing the play *Straight White Men*. Claiming paralysis is synonymous with saying there is nothing to be done. Taking the position that there is nothing to be done serves to maintain the existing structure—the White dominant structure. White folks of divided perspectives defend White dominance.

To be fair, there was also some backlash on the BET awards show from Asian Americans who were troubled by the cultural appropriations and fetishizing of Asians, when Asian costumes and music were part of the wardrobes and props for the song, "All The Way Up" by Fat Joe, Remy Ma and French Montana during their performance. Comedian Chris Rock also received criticism for being hypocritical when he hosted the Academy Awards. He devoted most of his monologue to highlight the racism in Hollywood, only to racialize his humor toward Asian children in a humorless skit. Some critics of this chapter would be quick to dismiss White 22 based on the premise that since everyone is racist, inconsistent, and hypocritical, we should stop only focusing on White people. Because White people continue to remain in dominant positions of privilege and power, we focus on White people and White 22. If our work was in the People's Republic of China, we would surely talk about the dominance of Han Chinese and Yellow privilege. A book on gender equity would most certainly have a chapter on Male 22 that captures the same concepts mentioned herein, with particular focus on gender. We (Collins and Jun) acknowledge our limitations on a discussion of gender equity as two heterosexual *cis*gendered Christian men. We have both experienced our fair share of times when we felt shut down just when we thought we were effectively engaging in efforts of solidarity with female colleagues. There is only *de facto* paralysis, and there is in fact much work for folks in a dominant group to do, but the first step is to sit down. Be quick to listen more and slow to speak. Be prepared to be a little uncomfortable. Allow critical consciousness to uproot the White architecture of the mind that leads to a defensive posture. Be slow to respond defensively to every challenge toward your efforts of solidarity. We hope that despite critiques, White allies would not give up. We hope you would continue to use your privilege wisely and intentionally in diversity related conversations within your spheres of influence.

## Notes

1. Goggans, Aaron, "Dear White people: Ferguson protests are a wake not a pep rally," last modified November 26, 2014, https://wellexaminedlife.com/2014/11/26/dear-white-people-ferguson-protests-are-a-wake-not-a-pep-rally/
2. Ibid.
3. Ulaby, Neda, "Straight white men," *A Play Explores the Reality of Privilege*, last modified November 17, 2014, http://www.npr.org/sections/codeswitch/2014/11/17/364760889/in-straight-white-men-a-play-explores-the-reality-of-privilege
4. Ibid.
5. Taylor, Edward. "A primer on critical race theory: who are the critical race theorists and what are they saying?" *The Journal of Blacks in Higher Education* 19 (1998): 122.
6. Corbett, Steve, and Brian Fikkert. *When helping hurts: How to alleviate poverty without hurting the poor ... and yourself.* Chicago: Moody Publishers, 2014.
7. DiAngelo, Robin, "White liberal racism: An interview with Dr. Robin DiAngelo," *The Huffington Post*, last updated on August 18, 2016, http://www.huffingtonpost.com/carol-smaldino/white-liberal-racism-an-i_b_11565484.html. See also, DiAngelo, Robin. "White fragility." *The International Journal of Critical Pedagogy* 3, no. 3 (2011).
8. Heron, Barbara. *Desire for development: Whiteness, gender, and the helping imperative.* Waterloo, Ontario: Wilfrid Laurier University Press, 2007. We find this book to be essential reading. It follows the recollections of White Canadian women who engaged in development work across the continent of Africa. Heron revealed how desire and identity is intertwined with race, class, and gender. There is a deep desire to be situated as doing good in the world and it requires an Other in need of help.
9. Kendall, Frances. *Understanding white privilege: Creating pathways to authentic relationships across race.* New York: Routledge, 2012.
10. Patton, Lori D., and Stephanie Bondi. "Nice white men or social justice allies?: using critical race theory to examine how white male faculty and administrators engage in ally work." *Race Ethnicity and Education* 18, no. 4 (2015): 488–514.
11. Thompson, Audrey. "Tiffany, friend of people of color: White investments in antiracism." *International Journal of Qualitative Studies in Education* 16, no. 1 (2003): 7–29.
12. Ibid.

13. Helms, Janet E., "Toward a model of White racial identity development," in *Black and White racial identity: Theory, research, and practice* (Santa Barbara, CA: Greenwood Press, 1990), 49–66.

14. Cabrera, Nolan L., Jesse S. Watson, and Jeremy D. Franklin. "Racial arrested development: A critical whiteness analysis of the campus ecology." *Journal of College Student Development* 57, no. 2 (2016): 119–134.

15. Ibid.

16. Lasher, Megan, "Read the full transcript of Jesse Williams' powerful speech on race at the BET awards," *TIME*, last modified June 27, 2016, http://time.com/4383516/jesse-williams-bet-speech-transcript/

17. Chan, Melissa, "Justin Timberlake sorry after angry response to Jesse Williams Tweet," *TIME*, last modified June 27, 2016, http://time.com/4383423/justin-timberlake-jesse-williams-speech/

18. Kane, Kim, "Dear Tomi Lahren: Take several seats," *Huffington Post*, last modified July 1, 2016, http://www.huffingtonpost.com/kim-kane/dear-tomi-lahren-take-several-seats_b_10760446.html

# Chapter Five

# Whitrogressions

## Now I'm the Victim

A colleague bemoaned to me (Jun) after I led a workshop that addressed the ongoing prevalence of microaggresisons at university campuses across the country, that he now felt like the victim of racism and micro-agressions as a White man. He shared how increasingly concerned he had become over what seemed to be acceptable racialized insults and bashing of White men in particular, without any consequence. "How come everyone can make fun of and pick on White men like me, and never be called racist?" he asked in frustration. "It's not fair," he concluded as he shook his head.

We have heard similar arguments like this in the past from White colleagues, students, and friends over the past several years: why is it okay to bash White people, but not people of color? White men are increasingly expressing feelings of being targeted and singled out and micro aggressed when discussing race relations. The term *microaggressions* has been around for several decades but was most recently defined by psychologist Derald Wing Sue[1] as he described racial microaggressions—brief and commonplace daily verbal, behavioral, or environmental indignities, whether intentional or unintentional, that communicate hostile, derogatory, or negative racial slights and insults toward people of color. I (Jun) have written about my own experiences with microaggressions within the evangelical Christian community.[2]

In this chapter, we explore microaggressions, the history of racial epithets toward White people, and the construction of Whitrogressions as another strategy of defending White dominance. In chapter six, Angry White Men, we address some of the consequences and byproducts that emerged out of this frustration of being *Whitroggressed* against by people of color. The ultimate aim of this chapter is to explore the development of Whitrogressions and the ways in which their history reveals a deeply imbedded sequence in the blueprints for the White architecture of the mind to defend White dominance. Whitrogrssions are verbal slights, racial slurs, and insults toward White people that do not have the same power and magnitude as macro or microaggressions toward people of color, but are taken with the same level of offense.

People of color and White people often perceive derogatory racial slurs toward White people differently. Those in the dominant group often claim that they are experiencing reverse racism as a result of what some perceive as an angry, politically correct, Marxist, anti-White, and anti-American agenda. Many who still fail to see color and defend White dominance through colorblind ideologies often find critiques of dominant systems to be very offensive, racist, and personally attacking. Some have expressed to us their fear of anarchy and overthrow of American values and beliefs. From our perspective, dominant groups cannot receive slurs and negative attitudes the same way as people of color because of the dissonance between these attitudes and the benefits that are typically associated with a dominant status.

## Microaggressions

An important precursor for this chapter is the concept and impact of microaggressions. The longer history and study of race has focused on overt racism and the infliction of derogatory terms. The defense of White dominance can be seen in relation to something overt like the use of the n[word]. The critique from White people is that using it should be acceptable for them since it is acceptable for use within the Black community. They then sense injustice and hypocrisy when told that it is not acceptable for use by White people. Although overt racism exists in many forms the expansion in understanding microforms has become both prominent and valuable. The earliest explanation from 1974 used the Black and White binary to highlight that,

> These assaults to black dignity and black hope are incessant and cumulative. Any single one may be gross. In fact, the major vehicle for racism in this country is offenses done to blacks by whites in this sort of gratuitous never-ending way. These offenses are microaggressions. Almost all black-white racial interactions are characterized by white put-downs, done in automatic, preconscious, or unconscious fashion. These mini-disasters accumulate. It is the sum total of multiple microaggressions by whites to blacks that has pervasive effect to the stability and peace of this world.[3]

We find the study and impact of microagressions essential to understanding race relations. Microforms of aggression and assault create hostile environments in which to work or study, they have real impacts on mental and physical health, lower productivity, and perpetuate inequities. Although a paper cut or bee sting may be a small injury, a mass accumulation of those small injuries over a lifetime is severe. The accumulative impact of microaggressions is like death by a thousand paper cuts. As the recognition of the impact of microaggressions expands, the resistance to acknowledging their impact also increases. As with other methods for defending White dominance, the ability to make similar claims in the White experience is to deprive the significance of the race-connected explanations of how people of color experience the world. Consequently, Whitrogressions are a claim to being the target of slurs and experiences in order to devalue the legitimacy of the experiences of people of color. Although there is a history of slurs toward White people, especially as it relates to class, the influence of power and privilege mitigate the impact of the verbal assaults.

# Outbreeding the Trash

Over the years many derogatory terms have been used to insult White people across regions in the United States. Indeed terms exist across cultures around the world. Negative descriptors such as cracker, honky, redneck, hillbilly, White boy, and White trash are just a few derogatory terms used to insult White people. Other terms, such as *haole*, gringo, Anglo, and Caucasian have been used as seemingly neutral descriptors of Whites but have also been seemingly co-opted terms that have led to feelings of Whitrogressions for some in the dominant group.

Although certain aspects of the term Whitrogression will highlight White fragility, the history of the White underclass in the US highlights another aspect of the concept—fear of losing dominance, even from within the White race. In the mid 1800s, the notions of imperial destiny and biological determinism were strong, and the idea that there was a superior "American blood" became prominent. As a result, the advancement of the race had to occur through selecting sexual partners of the same blood.[4] The frenzy became more "scientific" and evolved into eugenics, which is a social philosophy around improving human genetics through increasing sexual reproduction for desired traits and decreasing or sterilizing reproduction of undesirable traits. The Racial Integrity Act of 1924 proscribed interracial marriages. This law defined White as having no trace of any blood but Caucasian and was followed by a landmark decision in *Buck vs. Bell* giving the government the ability to regulate breeding among citizens. Chief Justice Oliver Wendell Holmes found sterilization to be a civic duty in order to filter out incompetence. Accordingly, the 1920s saw "social exclusiveness masquerade as science and disdain for rural backwardness."[5]

Nancy Isenberg, author of the book *White Trash*, argued that the use of derogatory terms for lower class Whites is a central narrative that proves an obsession in American society over labels we give to people we do not wish to notice. The history of the White underclass can be taken multiple ways. On one side it highlights the ways in which class plays a serious role in domination and oppression (similar to the primary topic of this project—race). As the White underclass was segregated into a separate race and sterilized out of fear of inbreeding, there are clear examples of the intersections and creations of class and race oppression. At the same time as the Racial Integrity Act were the Immigration Restriction Act of 1924 against southern and eastern European immigrants, and Deportation Act of 1929 against Mexicans. Italian and Irish immigrants were not considered White upon their arrival to the US, but Roediger demonstrated how they were able to achieve Whiteness.[6] It largely occurred through consorting with the dominant White race to make sure that people of color remained on the bottom of the hierarchy. The White underclass eventually benefited from this arrangement and found greater opportunities for social mobility. Eugenics, the history of White trash, and the legal construction of what it means to be White ultimately worked together to maintain a racial hierarchy.

We argue that the history of the construction of Whiteness began even before these 20th century. For example, well before the Racial Integrity Act, the US created immigration policies that required proving Whiteness for citizenship. These early immigration policies and then later exclusions acts that specifically excluded certain non-White races, such as the Chinese Exclusion Act, served as the foundation of constructing Whiteness as a US standard for inclusion, citizenship, and social power.

Whitrogressions may be interpreted as a slur and often feel painful, yet as stated earlier, the history of Whitrogressions reveals a deeply imbedded sequence in the blueprints for the White architecture of the mind, which is called upon knowingly or unknowingly to defend White dominance. In what follows we provide some Whitrogressive terms with brief explanations.

Cracker as a racial epithet has been in use for several hundred years. Comedian Chris Rock's comedy album, *Bigger and Blacker*, includes a sketch where he is depicting the dual nature of how a Black person may approach talking with someone who is White. Initially the tone is along the lines of, "How you doing, sir? Pleased to meet you. Whatever I can get you, you let me know." Then, Rock goes on to say,

> As soon as the White man get out of sight, he's like: 'Cracker-ass cracker! I'll put my foot in the crack of your ass, cracker-ass cracker! I wish that cracker would've said some shit to me, saltine-assed, motherfucking cracker!'[7]

Cracker has evolved into a White racial slur beginning as early as the 1700s and has been synonymous with interlopers, trespassers, and unpoliced squatters who took resources like crops, timber, animals, and fish from land they did not own. The term first appeared in British official records in the 1700s to describe lawless noisy braggers who were prone to lying, vulgarity, and who could "crack" a crude joke.[8] The lineage of the term evolved and was also considered applicable to poor White people who managed slaves but did not own land.

Leading up to the Civil War, the term squatter and cracker (as well as the concern for poor White people acting like Native Americans/ Indians) had faded from common use. The term poor White trash evolved as an enduring insult for the diseased and degenerate spawns of White folks.[9] In some ways, White trash southerners became a race of their own and had fallen below the status of other races. Some have been argued that the word emerged from the days of chattel slavery in the United States, for poor White field workers who cracked their whips. In 2006 Dana Ste. Claire wrote about the history of Crackers in Florida, found that the derogatory term referred to Celtic (Scotch Irish) immigrants who settled in the southeast part of the United States.[10] They were viewed as an unruly group with poor manners who lived off the land as homesteaders, and thus were looked down upon by broader society.

Honky as another White racial slur was arguably a derivative term for Hunky, a derogatory term for Hungarian immigrants in the early 1900's who were mostly poor low wage laborers and thus looked down upon in society. In the early days of society as white Europeans continued to arrive on U.S. shores derogatory terms for different nationalities were prevalent, but over time, as Roediger[11] and his colleague[12] pointed out, people of European ancestry slowly became White.

Redneck is a derogatory term rooted historically to insult poor White rural farmers in the south in the 19th century. In his book, Redneck Manifesto[13] author Jim Goad challenged the notion that racism can only come from people in power within a system. He argued that poor Whites are called rednecks and are the target of many jokes by all other ethnic groups with impunity. We agree that intentional verbal insults and racial slurs, including White people, are not only uncharitable but also demeaning. We also submit that a system of racism is nevertheless in place and perpetuated along the lines of a dominant group, and that well educated people of color for several generations in the United States, continue to experience structural discrimination based on race.

Haole, a term used first in the early 1800's by native people of Hawaii. Originally meant to describe any non-indigenous Hawaiian but now primarily refers to White people living in Hawaii. It had once been argued by Charles Kenn[14] that the term literally translated as "one without breath" in reference to the way European explorers were seen greeting one another without exchanging breaths, which was the traditional way native Hawaiians greeted one another. Although holding residence over time in Hawaii may afford White folks a special category, the term haole is tied to ongoing issues of sovereignty, colonization, and belonging. However, as many activists in Hawaii continue to fight for independence and sovereignty from White colonization that illegally occupied the island nation, the presence of White foreigners continues to be source of conflict and derision, and the word haole has been used to express this pain. Similarly, the word Gringo, which has Mexican roots and refers to White foreigners, has its origin in the Spanish word for Greek. The word has been used broadly to refer both positively and negatively, to U.S. citizens, Europeans, Latinos who speak little or no Spanish.

## The Problem with *Caucasian*

Caucasian has been used synonymously with White. Critics take exception with the word Caucasian.[15] The word literally references the mountainous Caucasus region near the independent nation of Georgia, and is problematic as a racial classification because the native people of that region are phenotypically not considered White. As a result it is some combination of ironic and ignorant to use this geographic term as the basis for White populations who typically would locate and associate their ancestry to Europe. An analysis of the word Caucasian in books shows a spike in use in the post civil rights era (see Figure 5.1). The rise in the use of the word corresponds with replacing the term Black with African American, making Caucasian an attempt at sounding like a neutral or dispassionate term for White.

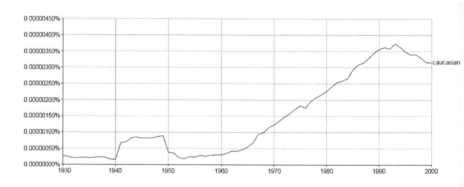

Figure 5.1. Use of the Word Caucasian in Books from 1930 to 2000

The term has its origins in the late 18th century when a couple of White men attempted to sound scientific in using skulls to construct views of race and beauty. The racist pseudo-science was used to support notions that Germans were the most beautiful of all people. Cranium measurements, weak anthropology, the search for beauty, and a hierarchy of races led to the creation and use of the term Caucasian, and it continues today. Even a Supreme Court justice used the word to describe a plaintiff in 2012.[16] In the end, the term has racist origins, inaccurate and ironic geographical/racial applications, and perpetuates a neutral view of race. As a result, common use of the term may serve to White Out the role and influence of understanding Whiteness. For those reasons, we find that the word is conflicted and should not be used when talking about White people and White systems.

# The N[word] for White People

Of all the negative terms, slanderous words and offensive comments levied against White people over the centuries, we have found that the one word that makes White people most defensive—*racist*. I (Collins) have suggested that the r[word] is the new n[word] for White people. Though we both recognize and acknowledge that any n[word] equivalent may not exist because no word can encapsulate 400 years of enslavement followed by legal maneuvering to perpetuate the poor treatment of former slaves through a series of Jim Crow laws. Defensive postures emerge and the White architecture of the mind is exposed whenever the word racist is invoked. A common defense tactic is one of two approaches. First response is a denial that one is personally racist. This reaction speaks perhaps to the individualistic nature of White people and culture in western society. The second is the opposite response that *everyone* is racist and therefore any claims of White people being racist are rejected. In terms of the defensive statement, I (Jun) had an interaction with someone who offered this ready defense of both arguments at the same time:

Everyone is racist. Not just members of the majority White race in America but everyone! I think that everyone from every culture can be racist, including minorities, especially when they exclude White people. How can there be minority only meetings and clubs like Black Student Unions, Asian only fraternities ad sororities, where no Whites are allowed? The radical idea of racial justice only oppresses White people. When scholarships are granted solely by race, again White people are excluded, and money is available only to minorities, Whites are now consistently denied funds to help with their studies. This is reverse racism. When minorities look at someone from the majority culture and assume that person got there by privilege, this is prejudice and racism. Some poor people will look at wealthy people and want what they want, and they can have it if they apply themselves and work hard! Others refused to work hard, they were scared to take risks and simply did not go as far in life. It has nothing to do with systemic racism. Now White people are being singled out and not part of the diversity conversation. Diversity means everyone is included except for White people. I have dedicated my life and the lives of my children to treat everyone the same and not to discriminate on the basis of color or creed. I am in a mixed race marriage and my wife has never been mistreated for not being White.

This exchange illustrates the Whitrogressions that some have been feeling over the years: the ongoing denial of systemic racism based on one's own personal lived experiences, through a dominant lens, and cries of reverse racism that presupposes an already post-racial and post-civil rights leveled playing field. Some of the statements from this individual are undergirded by a belief in a myth of meritocracy that tells White people that hard work, aspiration, and risk taking are the keys to success, which leaves people of color with only themselves to blame for their failures. A fundamental foundation for defending White dominance is to construct and support the belief that racism is possible everywhere and therefore less likely to occur anywhere. Eradicating or reducing the ability to be identified as a White racist further reduces the direction of the power dynamic and obfuscates the historical and systemic inequities. The desire to be a good White person can unintentionally apply White Out to the reality of racism.

## Becky and Shaniqua

A White person who refers to any Black woman as Shaniqua will most certainly be identified as making a racist comment that stereotypes and essentializes Black people. Much to the surprise of many White folks, the term Becky is a term used for White women in some Black spaces. The year 2016 reintroduced the racialized term as singer Beyoncé releasing her hit music video, Lemonade. Among the empowered, politically layered, and racially controversial themes, one provocative and highly publicized lyric is: "He better call Becky with the good hair." The Becky and Shaniqua comparison begged the question, is it racist for Black women to refer to White women as Becky?

Television host Wendy Williams[17] responded to the controversy by stating "Calling a white girl 'Becky' … is like calling a black girl 'Shaniqua.'" Others were quick to defend Beyoncé, acknowledging that while "Becky" is generally a negative descriptive term, it was not a racist epithet. Historically the name first appeared in William Makepeace Thackeray's 1847 novel, Vanity Fair.[18] Thackery's protagonist, Becky Sharp was portrayed as a social climber who used her charm to seduce men. Cara Kelly of USA Today[19] offered a brief history of Becky, from Thackery's 1847 novel to Mark Twain's 1876 novel Tom Sawyer, where Becky Thatcher seduces Tom. The name Becky appears in the 1992 music video Baby Got Back, by Sir Mix A Lot, where Becky is portrayed as a clueless White woman.

The name over time has become a reference to White women. Again, it is unclear to what extent White women have been either aware of or offended by the reference. Anecdotally, our experience with our White colleagues has been mixed, with perhaps much being dependent upon the degrees of exposure for White women to Black communities.

How does knowledge of these terms and their origins add or connect to the point we are making in the chapter? First we would argue that these derogatory words against White people have been around for generations, and have been used to insult and highlight differences. Many White people have invariably taken offense to these pejorative words at different times, and we would acknowledge there these are painful insults that should not be used. The challenge of Whitrogression is manifold. Any verbal insult that is conscious and intentional along the lines of race ought to be checked and corrected. However, the notion of an already leveled playing field that suggests that power has been well distributed and opportunities and merit are objective and symmetrical remains problematic.

To offer a brief summary here, we would once again acknowledge that many White people feel discriminated against today. We have made the case that Whitrogressions are not the same as microaggressions in that power and dominance in racist systems impacts minoritzed groups differently than those from a dominant majority group. We imagine that the ways in which the dominant group members react to Whitrogressions will indicate how there has been an ongoing lack of understanding about the connection between power and racial equality, and how many in a dominant group have long viewed society in terms of racial equality and leveled playing fields.

- What is the difference between a racial slur against a person of color and a racial slur against a White person? A racial slur against a person of color is a reach back into 400 years of systemized terrorism and racism against non-White members of American society. These racial slurs come with a history and with that history comes power. Whether the one speaking the words knows it or not, this historical oppressive power carries with it the perpetuation of White dominance, even through what may appear to some as a small offense.
- A racial slur against a White person is a slight against this oppressive system itself. Criticizing White people is a criticism of the White system that has been oppressive to people of color; a way of questioning and criticizing—or sometimes laughing at—the ways of being and acting that have created the dominantly White culture in which we find ourselves today.
- A microaggression against a person of color says, "Whether I know it or not, I am demonstrating power over you." Conversely a Whitrogression says, "I am challenging this White dominant system of power."

We offer these points as a way to help further explain the difference between microaggressions and Whitrogressions.

## A Way Forward

To be called racist is perhaps one of the most insulting of slights and offensive insults that can be levied against White people. In my own (Collins) experience I have worked hard to be a nice White guy to ensure that no one would ever refer to me as racist. A common response that I have heard from my (Jun) White friends, colleagues, and students, when challenged on their actions is immediate claims of identity over action (that is not who I am) rather than acknowledging acts that are racist. Some White responses to criticism rely on using the same language as people of color, which combined with stealing down pain, referenced in chapter two, serves to White Out the reality of asymmetrical experiences. We acknowledge that this work is complex. However, complexity is not the same as everything being symmetrical. Whitrogressions then is an important concept that acknowledges the verbal insults toward individuals, while also challenging the notion that any critique toward dominant White systems of racism are still necessary and in need of greater interrogation.

## Notes

1. Sue, Derald Wing. *Microaggressions in everyday life: Race, gender, and sexual orientation.* Hoboken, NJ: John Wiley & Sons, 2010.

2. Jun, Alexander. "Unintentional Racism," in *Heal us, Emmanuel: A call for racial reconciliation, representation, and unity in the church,* ed. Doug Serven (Oklahoma City: Black White Bird Press, 2016), 21–26.

3. Pierce, Chester. "Psychiatric problems of the Black minority." *American handbook of psychiatry* 2 (1974): 512–523.

4. Isenberg, Nancy. *White Trash: The 400-year untold history of class in America.* New York: Penguin, 2016.

5. Ibid. 205.

6. Roediger, David R. *Working toward whiteness: How America's immigrants became white: The strange journey from Ellis Island to the suburbs.* New York: Basic Books, 2006.

7. Rock, Chris. *Bigger and Blacker* (DVD). HBO Studios (1999).

8. Isenberg, Nancy. *White Trash.*

9. Ibid.

10. Claire, Dana Ste. *Cracker: the Cracker culture in Florida history.* Gainesville, FL: University Press of Florida, 2006.

11. Roediger, *Working toward whiteness.*

12. Barrett, James R., and David Roediger. "How white people became white." *White Privilege In White Privilege: Essential Readings on the Other Side of Racism,* ed. Paula S. Rothenberg. New York: Worth Publishers, (2002): 29–34.

13. Goad, Jim. *The Redneck Manifesto: How Hillbillies Hicks and White Trash became America's scapegoats.* Simon and Schuster, 1998.

14. Kenn, Charles W. "What is a Haole?" *Paradise of the Pacific* (August 1944): 16.

15. Khan, Razib. "Stop using the word 'Caucasian' to mean white," *Discover Magazine,* last revised January 22, 2011, http://blogs.discovermagazine.com/gnxp/2011/01/stop-using-the-word-caucasian-to-mean-white/#.V6DyOpOAOko

16. Dewan, Shaila, "Has 'Caucasian' lost its meaning?" *New York Times*, last revised July 6, 2013, http://www.nytimes.com/2013/07/07/sunday-review/has-caucasian-lost-its-meaning.html?_r=0

17. Williams, Wendy, "Rita Ora the Real 'Becky'?!" *The Wendy Williams Show*, Last modified April 26, 2016, https://www.youtube.com/watch?v=QCM22u6gFVQ

18. Thackeray, William Makepeace. *Vanity fair*. Wordsworth Editions, 1992.

19. Kelly, Cara, "What does Becky mean? Here's the history behind Beyoncé's 'Lemonade' lyric that sparked a firestorm," *USA Today*, last revised April 27, 2016 http://www.usatoday.com/story/life/entertainthis/2016/04/27/what-does-becky-mean-heres-history-behind-beyoncs-lemonade-lyric-sparked-firestorm/83555996/

# Chapter Six

# Angry White Men: Making America White Again

On the evening of June 17, 2015, Dylann Roof entered a Bible study at the Emmanuel African Methodist Episcopal (AME) Church in Charleston, South Carolina. Roof sat down, prayed, read the Bible, and then killed nine Black Americans. Only one person was left alive, so she could tell the world what he had done and why—Roof said, "You're taking over our country."[1] He was a 21-year-old White high school dropout who used violence to recapture something that he felt he was losing. Although Dylann Roof did not have a formal education, he was actively learning from a variety of websites, including the Council of Conservative Citizens, which has roots in the 1950s White Citizens' Council that terrorized Black people, schools, and churches.[2] He wore a jacket with the colonial flag of White-ruled Rhodesia, which existed next to apartheid-era South Africa.

As with many killings committed by White men, a mental health explanation of his actions was quickly deployed to dissociate his actions with the fabric of White America. His actions were connected to being deranged and uneducated. Although he lacked formal education, he had been consuming a curriculum from the fabric of an angry subset of White America. Less than a month after this massacre, the eventual Republican presidential nominee Donald Trump spoke to an enthusiastic and mostly White audience with the primary promise, "Don't worry, we'll take our country back."[3]

## "Angry White Guys..."

The sentiment behind "taking the country back" has a deep historical legacy, especially as it relates to law and policy. In 2008, Barack Obama had been elected to be the first Black president of the United States of America. Around the world, the event was heralded as a victory for people of color and humanity at large. In some circles, the election was seen as the first event in a post-racial era for the US. Conversely, there was a great deal of dismay among political conservatives about what had occurred. Voter turnout analyses showed that, for the first time in history, the Black voting rate nearly equaled that of Whites, and that the only demographic sector that opponent John McCain dominantly won was with elderly White people and evangelical Christians.[4] The demographic voting results contributed to extensive political strategizing, but Republican Senator Lindsey Graham of South Carolina summarized the core of the issue when he said, "We're not generating enough angry White guys to stay in business for the long term."[5]

The historical legacy of the feeling of losing dominant White status started long before Obama was elected as President. It did not begin with the looming racial minority majority demographic shift in the US—the moment when people of color will comprise 51% of the population. As carefully outlined by Carol Anderson, White rage is not just about physical violence, but also the way it works through the courts, legislatures, bureaucracies, and educational systems. According to Anderson, the fuel for White rage is fear of Black advancement, and even historical heroes in the US took part. For example, famed President Abraham Lincoln once stated, "I am not, nor ever have been, in favor of bringing about in any way the social and political equality of the white and black races," which included opposition to voting, serving on juries, holding public office, or marrying across races.[6] Lincoln's disposition resulted in the resettling of large amounts of free Black people in Liberia and attempts to send them to colonize Panama. He told Black leaders that the war in the US would not have happened if it were not for their race.

After Obama was elected in 2008, many wondered if the US was entering a post racial era. At the end of his presidency in 2016, an entirely new and energized White anger emerged to overtly defend White dominance. For example, a billboard appeared on a Tennessee road that said, "MAKE AMERICA WHITE AGAIN." In an article accompanying the same image that was on the sign, candidate Rick Tyler argued for protecting White values by stopping all non-White immigration and maximizing immigration from Rhodesia (the correct name is Zimbabwe) and South Africa.[7] Rick Tyler is not a mainstream candidate, but his advocacy represents a level of overt attitudes that are making their way into the mainstream discourse. Shortly after the Republican National Convention nominated Donald Trump as their presidential candidate, David Duke, a former KKK leader, cited Trump's candidacy as an inspiration during his announcement to run for an open US Senate seat. He stated: "We must stop the massive immigration and ethnic cleansing of people whose forefathers created America."[8]

## Building Walls

Donald Trump's candidacy grew rapidly in significance. The mere chanting of "Trump! Trump! Trump!" has been used to invoke racial degradation. The public rhetoric by Trump, his campaign, and his broad coalition of supporters have been characterized by demeaning Mexican immigrants and promises to build a wall, broad generalizations of Muslims and promises to stop immigration, as well as myriad other comments about women and minorities. After a Black Lives Matter protester was attacked at a Trump rally, Trump indicated, "Maybe he should have been roughed up because it was absolutely disgusting what he was doing."[9] There is a renewed sense of the way White anger can play a role in the public square and on college campuses. The New York Times reported:

> On campuses clenched by unforgiving debates over language and inclusion, some students embrace Mr. Trump as a way of rebelling against the intricate rules surrounding privilege and microaggression, and provoking the keepers of those rules.[10]

Trump has given license to a privileged majority that is working diligently to co-opt minority arguments. The fact that some in the White majority do not feel privileged gives credence to the notion that, for the privileged, justice feels like oppression. Even a White nationalist in Montana argued that Trump facilitated identity politics for White people in a way that has never been done before.[11] On college campuses, the word Trump has been used in ways that are being called hate speech and in conjunction with chants like "Build that wall!"

The US political climate is not isolated. What is happening on college campuses and with the Trump campaign is connected to events around the world. The tension around immigration is a global phenomenon and the rhetoric infused into racialized notions of immigration is fueling tension around the world. One of the most significant global events of 2016 was Brexit—Britain's exit from the European Union. Many of the primary instigators behind the campaign to leave the European Union faded from public view after the *Leave* vote won, but Theresa May took over as Prime Minister when David Cameron stepped down. She noted that one of the primary messages in the Leave vote was to reduce immigration.[12] Even Trump connected his campaign to Brexit by emphasizing that people want their country back. The vote in Britain may be an indicator of global anxiety about immigration, a renewal of xenophobia, and a growing White rage. If what happened in Britain is a growing global sentiment, it may have been an early indicator that Trump would ultimately win the US presidency.

Moving beyond the overt and populist nature of the Trump movement, the liberal democratic side of the political range also illuminates some aspects of suppressed White anger. Hillary Clinton was the 2016 democratic presidential nominee, but she ran a tough campaign against Barack Obama in 2008. During the campaign, her husband Bill Clinton made some racially laced comments about Obama and was criticized accordingly. Much of Hillary's 2016 campaign was built around her status as woman candidate, including the slogan, "I'm with her." Her candidacy has consistently been depicted as breaking the highest glass ceiling for women. Ironically, this ignores or uses White Out over the fact that she is a White woman. Instead of being a White woman, she is just a woman, which propels White normativity that all women are White. An edited volume from 1982 is an early collection of essays that disrupts this normativity—it is entitled: *All the Women are White, All the Blacks Are Men, But Some of Us Are Brave: Black Women's Studies*.[13] The manifestation is that Hillary Clinton is always presented as the first woman (not White woman) to be the nominee of a major party. Barack Obama will always be the first Black president.

However, long before Hillary Clinton or Barack Obama was Shirley Chisholm; she is not well known, but was the first Black woman to be a member of congress and the first woman to run for President in the Democratic primary. Her campaign slogan was "Unbought and Unbossed" and she is quoted as saying, "If they don't give you a seat at the table, bring a folding chair."[14] Chisholm was radical, groundbreaking, and disconnected from the White Male political establishment. Much of the fanfare around Hillary Clinton's candidacy has done little to acknowledge Chisholm's role in US politics. Although Trump evoked and invoked White anger in and around his campaign, Hillary Clinton may have been powerful for White feminism and less favorable for racial justice.[15]

On November 9, 2016, Donald Trump was announced as the winner of the US Presidential election after an Electoral College victory (Hillary Clinton won the popular vote). Various analyses of the voting demographics showed that Trump drastically won the vote of White people without a college degree, White men, and White evangelical Christians.[16] The election came as shock after most polls showed Clinton winning. Van Jones of CNN was visibly upset on air and called the election *Whitelash* against a Black president.[17] Because of Trump's numerous comments about China, people from Mexico, Muslims, people with disabilities, the Black community, his election came as not only a surprise to many, but a included a feeling that of lacking safety. It is not just that Trump was elected, but that so many people support his

Presidency either because of his comments or in spite of them. Either way, the wave of angry White men made a concrete move to not only make America White again, but to reveal how dominantly White it is.

## White Occupiers and White Student Unions

In the state of Oregon in January 2016, some White anti-government ranchers broke into a federally owned wildlife refuge and committed to staying there until the government ended tyranny.[18] The background to this event includes a history of resisting the federal governments oversight of land in the Western US, grazing rights, fences, and even arson. After the occupation of the refuge started, other anti-government demonstrators joined from around the country and found ways to send supplies. Law enforcement and the government were slow to respond, which lead to the critique that if these were Muslim protestors or even the Black Lives Matter movement, they would have faced greater penalties more quickly.[19] The protestors stayed for 41 days and often spoke to the press. Previously, key organizer Cliven Bundy articulated that Black Americans might have been better off enslaved, perhaps as a way of highlighting how bad they believe the government to be. Most of the occupiers and all of the 23 men and women arrested for felony chargers were White.

If the story seems odd, it is. The history of federal land management and Western ranchers is complicated and increasingly tense. We include the event here because it is another example of overt and growing White anger from people who feel like they are losing something. It is an indication of the lengths to which White folks who feel like they need to resist will go to defend their dominance. Although there were relatively few occupiers in this demonstration, the levels of encouragement, support, and resources they received from across the US is at least an indication of a growing sentiment.

On college campuses, the resistance against growing attention to and around diversity and multiculturalism is articulated through the establishment of White Student Unions. At the University of California Santa Barbara (UCSB), University of Texas Austin, University of

Illinois, Penn State, University of Missouri, and several other universities, White Student Unions have been established. The philosophies and activities of these student groups have been documented on social media, with some of them garnering almost 1,000 "likes" on Facebook. Each of these groups *follow* the activity of other unions and share information about the perceived indoctrination of college students with liberal perceptions of race. When the UCSB White Student Union first emerged, it was largely deemed a mockery of the Black Lives Movement. The origin of the union included a list of demands that mimicked the demands of BLM protestors on campuses around the country. Since then, the group has continued and appears to have an active membership with events, activities, and discussions on the Facebook page. The group includes a description:

> The White Student Union of University of California, Santa Barbara exists to create a safe, supportive and inclusive student community of European descent. By providing opportunities for all students to increase awareness of European culture with an emphasis on European social, political, and intellectual traditions.[20]

A traditional White response to multicultural clubs has been, "Why don't we have a White Student Union" and a similar response asking about a White History Month. The proliferation of White Student Unions is another indicator of the growing force behind White Anger and the recapturing of something perceived as lost.

## White Christmas

Anger and frustration are emotions that are demonstrated in the sacred realms as well as the secular. I (Jun) have seen some of this anger emerge from White men and women in faith-based communities as well. For example, in the wake of a resolution on racial reconciliation and repentance for past and present racism within the denomination, adopted in 2016 by the theologically conservative Presbyterian Church in America (PCA), an anonymous White supremacist hate group has emerged. Calling for the end of inter-racial marriage, separation of races in churches, and fearing the demise of churches into liberal apostasy, this angry white separatist group, representing themselves as Christians, seek to dismantle the slow but steady work of racial justice within evangelical circles. Having spoken at and conducted workshops for different Christian colleges and organizations as well as for nonsectarian institutions, I have seen little difference in the responses from White people. Both secular and sacred institutions have reacted similarly, and often with resistance and anger, when presented with ideas about systemic racism, white privilege, and a need for racial justice. It troubles me greatly as one who identifies as a Christian, that while I ought to have more in common with what is most central to the core of my being with my White evangelical counterparts, the reality is, at least concerning issues of race and racism, that my White evangelical brothers and sisters seem to have more in common with their White agnostic neighbors. Jesus of Nazareth was a Jewish carpenter from the Middle East. Most of the apostles and early church founders were from Israel-Palestine. As the Christian faith spread slowly to White European gentiles over the course of several centuries, it is interesting to note the shift in iconography and rhetoric of a White Jesus and celebrations such as Christmas that includes syncretistic practices such the inclusion of tree decorations as art of high holy days of Christmas. While some of these practices seem to have strayed far from the original faith practices, they have been reified as part of Christian practice in the west. We intend to explore the role of Whiteness, fragility, and resistance in another forthcoming writing project, but for now, we note that evangelical Christianity in the North America today is still dominantly white.

## "I Don't Know..."

On July 20, 2016, police in North Miami received a call that someone had a gun.[21] Armed and ready, police officers approached Charles Kinsey, a behavioral therapist who was sitting on the ground assisting an autistic patient with a toy truck. Lying on his back on the ground, with his hands raised in the air, Kinsey was caught on video explaining clearly and loudly that he was a behavioral therapist and that his patient only had a toy truck. A police officer shot Kinsey, an unarmed Black man, in his leg and arrested him. Although it was not captured on video, Kinsey told reporters that he asked the officer why he shot him, and the officer replied, "I don't know." It is an incredibly unfortunate scenario to shoot an unarmed Black man in July of 2016, which falls in line with a litany of high profile shootings by police and on police. However, I (Collins) know why the officer shot Kinsey. I know, because the same logic system that helped form the architecture of his mind also shaped mine.

Basic anxiety is a psychological term for the fight or flight instinct that causes people to react in a certain way when in the presence of danger. Neurotic anxiety is driven by a disordered fear and actually blocks normal anxiety and self-awareness. The construction of fear outside of basic anxiety and the accumulation of anxious feelings around a particular issue may have a herding effect. In behavioral economics, herding is the attraction to something when there is a group of people surrounding it (e.g., a popular place to eat, street performer, or new version of a smart phone). Self-herding is the idea that the number of times you think about buying a new item is working toward a herd of decisions that construct desire around that item.[22] By the time you make the decision to purchase it, you mentally see a herd around the item, representing you and your thoughts about making the purchase—thereby self-herding.

## A Way Forward

A socially constructed fear about Black men becomes a fixture in White systemic thinking and fuels the White architecture of the mind. A normal setting in which there is no threat (therefore no basic anxiety) becomes altered when neurotic anxiety takes over. As self-awareness decreases, repeated and fear-driven neurotic anxiety becomes self-herded in a direction; a sub or unconscious decision is guided by neurotic anxiety. The cumulative weight of fear produces an irrational response. The phenomenon of angry White men is not limited to overtures about race and exclusion. The combination of feelings of loss and neurotic anxiety exists in a volatile space in the White architecture of the mind. It is not only about individual feelings and actions, but also about the accumulation of feelings among Angry White men dispersed across a country and even the world in a way that supports White dominance. These feelings can occur even when an individual does not know what drove their behavior or understand their actions.

We opened this chapter with the example of Dylann Roof, who was arrested the day after his mass shooting and subsequently placed with a protective vest and taken through a drive through window at a fast food restaurant (compared to the litany of unarmed Black men who have been shot recently). When we observe the disturbing action, events, and commentary presented in this chapter, we feel drawn to one of two approaches. The first is to isolate negative and neurotic behavior as a personal or individual problem. The draw of this approach is to alleviate ourselves from responsibility to someone's outwardly racist behavior. A second approach implies a more collective responsibility. In this approach, we see a tragedy like the shooting at the AME church in South Carolina as a symptom of a larger societal ill that inhabits all of our minds and bodies. In this approach, we resist the temptation to assign that action to one person so that we can look at the larger systematic feelings of loss and anxiety that are producing that Angry White man disposition that is required to maintain forms of dominance. We name and identify the phenomenon of Angry White Men in order to see society more clearly. Angry White Men are not so much a group of people as it is a spreading sentiment around the world to recapture a sense of what has been lost—namely dominant Whiteness. Extensive political, educational, and violent means will be used to preserve entitlements. By seeing the phenomenon more clearly, we intend to use education to demonstrate the ways in which the sentiment is constructed, acknowledge the way we play a role, and ultimately engage in deconstruction and decolonization.

# Notes

1. Dylann Roof's Racist Manifesto: "I have no choice." June 20, 2015, https://www.washingtonpost.com/national/health-science/authorities-investigate-whether-racist-manifesto-was-written-by-sc-gunman/2015/06/20/f0bd3052-1762-11e5-9ddc-e3353542100c_story.html
2. Anderson, Carol. *White Rage: The unspoken truth of racial divide*, London: Bloomsbury Publishing, 2016.
3. Trump, Donald. "Don't worry, we'll take our country back." July 11, 2015 http://www.nbcnews.com/politics/2016-election/donald-trump-freedomfest-you-cant-be-great-if-you-dont-n390546
4. How Groups Voted in 2008, Roper Center, http://ropercenter.cornell.edu/polls/us-elections/how-groups-voted/how-groups-voted-2008/
5. As Republican convention emphasizes diversity, racial incidents intrude. August 29, 2012, https://www.washingtonpost.com/politics/2012/08/29/b9023a52-f1ec-11e1-892d-bc92fee603a7_story.html
6. Anderson, p. 14.
7. Make America White Again. July 18, 2016, http://ricktylerforcongress.com/2016/07/18/make-america-white-again/
8. Former KKK leader David Duke, citing Trump, announces Senate bid. July 22, 2016, https://www.washingtonpost.com/news/powerpost/wp/2016/07/22/former-kkk-leader-david-duke-citing-trump-announces-senate-bid/#
9. Trump on protester: 'Maybe he should have been roughed up' November 23, 2015. *CNN*. http://www.cnn.com/2015/11/22/politics/donald-trump-black-lives-matter-protester-confrontation/
10. For Whites Sensing Decline, Donald Trump Unleashes Words of Resistance. July 13, 2016. *New York Times*. http://www.nytimes.com/2016/07/14/us/politics/donald-trump-white-identity.html
11. Ibid.
12. Brexit: All you need to know about the UK leaving the EU. July 21, 2016. BBC. http://www.bbc.com/news/uk-politics-32810887
13. Hull, G.T., P.B. Scott, and B. Smith (eds.) *All the women are white, all the blacks are men, but some of us are brave: Black women's studies*. Old Wesibury, NY: Feminist Press, 1982.
14. Before Clinton, Hillary. "There was Shirley Chisholm." *BBC News*. January 26, 2016. http://www.bbc.com/news/magazine-35057641
15. Daniels, Jessie. *Hillary Clinton: Good for white feminism, bad for racial justice*. April 12, 2015, http://www.racismreview.com/blog/2015/04/12/hillary-clinton-good-for-white-feminism

16. Alec Tyson and Shiva Maniam, Behind Trump's victory: Divisions by race, gender, education. *Pew Research Center*, November 9, 2016, http://www.pewresearch.org/fact-tank/2016/11/09/behind-trumps-victory-divisions-by-race-gender-education/

17. Josiah Ryan. "'This was a whitelash': Van Jones' take on the election results," *CNN*, November 9, 2016, http://www.cnn.com/2016/11/09/politics/van-jones-results-disappointment-cnntv/

18. Oregon standoff: All occupiers surrender; Cliven Bundy arrested. *CNN*, February 22, 2016, http://www.cnn.com/2016/02/11/us/oregon-standoff/

19. The Oregon Standoff, Black Lives Matter, and Criminal-Justice Reform. *The Atlantic*, January 5, 2015, http://www.theatlantic.com/national/archive/2016/01/the-oregon-standoff-debate/422556/

20. UCSB White Student Union. https://www.facebook.com/UCSB-White-Student-Union-685020354966554/

21. Chokshi, N. (July 21 2016). North Miami Police Officers Shoot Man Aiding Patient With Autism. *New York Times*. Retrieved from: http://www.nytimes.com/2016/07/22/us/north-miami-police-officers-shoot-man-aiding-patient-with-autism.html?_r=0

22. Ariely, D. *Predictably irrational: The hidden forces that shape our decisions.* New York: Harper Collins, 2008.

# Chapter Seven

# White Pilgrims at Thanksgiving

It happens every year at family gatherings across the country. Loved ones join together for Thanksgiving to a share a meal and celebrate the good work that the pilgrims achieved in their pursuit toward liberty. Invariably, however, some beloved relative might offer an alternative historical account of U.S. history, which leads to a heated debate about gun control, affirmative action, or police brutality. Oftentimes, discussions like these are poorly timed and can become so heated that Thanksgiving dinner becomes more like a contact sport than the annually televised football game. Thanksgiving dinners are oftentimes a *safe space* where mostly racially homogenous families with long histories can speak freely without fear of retribution. This has certainly been the case for both of our (Jun and Collins) Thanksgiving family dinners: until we integrated with mixed race family members by marriage and/ or adoption.

This chapter's title is a play on words meant to highlight the conversations that occur among racially homogenous friends and family members with whom people are close. As such, the notion of Pilgrims at Thanksgiving is a reminder that pilgrims are clearly in the dominant group. They were the White settlers: they could speak freely at the table as they ate the natural resources taken from someone else's land.

For generations, citizens in the United States have been celebrating this act. People take time off work so that they can go home, unbutton the top button on their pants, only eat the white meat, and then speak freely about people of color. These conversations can occur with many people beyond family: they can occur with neighbors, among fraternity or sorority members, within churches and synagogues, and with colleagues, supervisors, or direct reports at work. Upon hearing provocative statements, people might be troubled by what was said, and troubled by how best to respond. After all, nobody wants to jeopardize a good relationship, add to an already awkward situation, or compromise Thanksgiving.

The approach for this chapter is slightly different than the others; we turn our attention to some common conversation topics that might emerge among loved ones, friends, classmates, and co-workers. Family dinners and other impromptu gatherings of racially homogenous groups might be considered safe spaces for people to say something that they might not say in other settings because they know they can get away with it. The question that drives this chapter is simply: How can we deal with and handle hard conversations with people we care about? With the aid of some friends and colleagues who share real life examples, we offer some possible solutions as well as some resources to help guide the reader to extend the conversation beyond a single isolated interaction. Each situation includes an example of the defensive statement, context for the conversation, an explanation of the problem with the statement, and an example of how it was disrupted or deconstructed.

## Whites Are the New Slaves

"Blacks and Mexicans get everything for free
and off the sweat of our backs. We are the new slaves."

**Context:** At a party, the subject of welfare came up. Immediately, Grant began a tirade about how whites are the "new slaves," while "Blacks and Mexicans get everything for free and off the sweat of our backs."

He reiterated that White people have to work and pay for everything, while Black people and Mexicans sit at home collecting welfare checks and free food that they did not earn or deserve. He said he was tired of knowing his paychecks are taxed to give them the ability to stay home and be a parasite. Grant claimed he was not racist and had a few Black friends, but that he was tired of racism against Whites people. Grant then spoke at length about illegal immigration and how his friends have difficulty finding construction jobs because "the Mexicans steal all the jobs on top of using up all the welfare." He continually defended his position by saying that he was the victim of racism, not the other way around. When Sam countered with examples of racism and mentioned how the definition of the word makes it impossible for it to apply for him, he kept repeating that he was not racist and that he has "Black friends and even voted for Obama."

**Problem:** In addition to Grant's argument being inaccurate, lacking logic, and offensive, it was clear that he was unwilling to listen to alternative opinions or accept facts that countered his statements. For example, he mentioned that high schools and colleges have clubs for ethnicities, but if he wanted to start a Caucasian club, he would not be able to. However, for majority culture White students, most clubs, activities, and organizations, like Greek fraternity and sorority houses, are geared toward White students, so separate groups would simply be redundant. A separate White Student Union to counter the Black Student Union would be duplicating efforts, because the student union has long been a space for majority culture White folks.

**Disruption:** In conversation with Grant, Sam asked if he was serious about believing White people are slaves: Grant responded affirmatively. Although Sam provided information about slavery and described how slaves were whipped, tortured, pulled away from families, hunted and often killed when trying to escape, and viewed as property in lieu a being a whole person, Grant continued to resist. He became defensive and said that White people are being forced to work to provide for others, which is what slavery was about. Even when Sam mentioned data and statistics on welfare (e.g., White people comprise 38.8% of welfare recipients) and described how institutional racism is structurally built into government, media, and education, Grant remained unconvinced. Despite Grant's unwillingness to entertain Sam's viewpoint and or yield to the statistics, Sam's response was justified and likely made an impact on others who were listening but had not contributed to the conversation.

## Lighthearted Racism

"It's not that big of a deal, can't they just take a joke?"
"They're so sensitive; we don't mean anything by it."

**Context:** Marty, a White student, was sitting with a group of four Australian high school boys, two who are White, one who presents as White but has Aboriginal heritage that the others might not know about, and one who is Black. The boys were casually talking in their unit at a boarding school when Marty said that marginalized people do not really have it that bad and should not whine so much and expect everything to be politically correct. Marty also reiterated that jokes made at the expense of marginalized people are just jokes, and any offensiveness taken is because they are too sensitive.

**Problem:** This example represents an excuse or defense of White dominance, White privilege, and perhaps male privilege. For example, who gets to decide when people are whining or if their concern is legitimate? Does the dominant group get to decide when the marginalized group is being too sensitive, even though the dominant group has never experienced what the marginalized group is experiencing?

**Disruption:** A mentor disrupted the conversation by asking a question and speaking in a very measured, calm, and respectful way that was neither loud nor passionate. With a somewhat didactic disposition, the mentor asked Marty to consider a hypothetical situation:

> Imagine a party and most of the people at that party were wealthy, but some of the people were poor, poverty-stricken, and homeless. What would it be like if the wealthy started making fun of the poor for the rags they wore, or the homes they live in, or their lifestyles?

Marty's response was immediate and obvious: "That would be hurtful, ridiculous, and shouldn't happen."

The mentor continued:

> What if the poor people then responded to the taunts by complaining that they were being mistreated by the wealthy and then the wealthy proceeded to malign the poor people for being too sensitive, not being able to take a joke, or expecting something to be politically correct?

Marty's response was perhaps obvious: "the rich would be wrong for berating the poverty-stricken and homeless for being too sensitive."

Although the mentor's point was made without much further explanation, he made another point more explicitly without a story or analogy. He shared that he does not believe the dominant group should ever get to decide when the marginalized group is being too sensitive. How can the dominant group who has never experienced that particular marginalization claim to be entitled to an opinion? Only those who are marginalized (in the case of the mentor's made-up allegory it would be other similarly poor people) can help other marginalized decide when they are being too sensitive or responding inappropriately.

## Affirmative Action

"I'm sorry, but we can't hire the person who is best qualified
for the job, we have to hire an African American?"

**Context:** While enjoying the Thanksgiving holiday with extended family, a conversation emerged around a situation at Charlotte's workplace. Charlotte shared that several people applied for a position in her office and her boss told her that there were many qualified people. Her boss also noted that they had to hire an African American. Charlotte's response was one of frustration:

> Wait, I'm sorry, but we can't hire the person who is best qualified for the job, we have to hire an African American? So we hired the African American and he is terrible! It's not good for him or for us, and we should only hire the most qualified person for the job.

**Problem:** There is a distinct possibility that Charlotte was overgeneralizing. Did her boss really talk about this confidential personnel situation with all of his staff and let them know that he thought this applicant was not qualified? Is the new hire actually not qualified? Were there really several qualified White applicants and this one African American man was much less qualified than the other White applicants? In short, when faulty logic does not include all the facts, it essentializes and stereotypes Black applicants. Charlotte also didn't articulate an understanding of the need to diversify or how diversity could benefit the company, nor did she express an understanding of the complicating factors that have led to there being a majority of White applicants for the job.

**Disruption:** Charlotte asked her sister Sarah if she actually thought that it was better to hire an unqualified African American and turn down a qualified White person. Sarah noted that she did not think the question was as easy and straightforward as it was presented. Sarah explained that one of the reasons for legal diversification efforts and standards is because of the legal segregation that existed for decades. She reminded Charlotte that laws used to legally permit White people to take away rights and limit access based on race (e.g., Jim Crow laws, redlining, GI Bill and home ownership, etc.).

Solutions are challenging when something like racial exclusion, which has a complex, multi-layered, and long-lasting societal impact, is the bedrock of a country. Simple black and white answers (e.g., "just hire the most qualified person") will probably not suffice. For example, what does "most qualified" mean? Whose definition of "most qualified" is being used? As a way to explain the complexity of these questions, Sarah described studies that have experimented with submitting identical resumes for jobs, with some having names that others may perceive as being associated with a certain race to see which resumes receive the most call backs. These studies have shown that resumes with names that others may perceive as being associated with African Americans were much less likely to get a call for an interview than those resumes that had names that others may perceive as being associate with Whites.

# But Black People Are Intimidating

"I don't want to sound ignorant or anything, but Black people
can be intimidating."

**Context:** This statement emerged in a conversation between Harold, a
19-year-old biracial (Black and White) intern and his supervisor, Tanya,
the day after Alton Sterling and Philando Castile were killed in July
2016. As a Black woman struggling and hurting with the news, Tanya
wanted to see how her only Black intern was coping and provide him
a safe space to work through these challenging times. However, when
Harold walked into her office, he did not intend to discuss the current
societal climate: he planned to talk about a young lady he liked. When
Tanya asked if he was ok, she realized that Harold was unaware of the
shootings. After they viewed the videos that showed Sterling and Castile's deaths, he sat in silence.

**Problem:** Harold's statement illustrates the continuous perpetuation
of prejudice and judgment against Black people, even from within the
Black community. His supervisor found it especially troubling that Harold seemed to agree that Black people are threatening and hostile who
might deserve to be killed, regardless of their infraction. Tanya sensed
that this bi-racial young man's image, which is part of his lineage, has
been distorted and internalized. Harold does not connect very much
with other Black men on campus and his closest friends are non-Black.

Although Harold might have felt justified for making the statement
because he is half Black, the comment was racist; Tanya wondered who
taught him to see the world this way—the Black side of his family or
the White side? Nonetheless, he was unaware and unconscious of this
critical issue in society. Moreover, Harold's circle of friends, and perhaps a broader majority of students on campus were also unaware and
insulated—so much so that none of these videos were showing up on
their social media feeds to even spark conversations.

**Disruption:** After staring at her intern in silence for several minutes,
Tanya called Harold by name and asked, "If all African Americans are
intimidating, am I intimidating to you?" Her goal was for him to see

the error in generalizing and stereotyping an entire group of people. She also suggested alternatives to the police killing Black men (e.g., giving a citation, arresting and/or tasing, or even non-lethal shooting in the leg if police actually felt their life was danger). Harold responded that these men should not have committed crimes in the first place. Tanya agreed that it is ideal to stay away from behaviors that would invite police attention, but acknowledged that it is not that simple. She also verbalized that minor traffic infractions should never equate to death at the hands of those who are called to protect and serve.

## Be Ye Not Unequally Yoked

*"Because the Bible forbids interracial marriage."*

**Context:** When James was a junior in high school, a group of church friends started a band that eventually led worship for their Christian church high school group. The Black keyboardist, Richard, expressed an interest in asking James's sister Kathy out on a date. James was excited about the prospect, because Richard was a good guy and Kathy had just ended a relationship with a jerk. James gave Richard his "blessing" and he asked her out. Kathy initially said yes to Richard, but the next night at dinner when Kathy told their parents about the potential date, they quickly and harshly forbade her from going. They offered no explanation at first, but when pushed, they explained that it was dangerous and maybe even unbiblical for people of different races to marry.

**Problem:** James and Kathy's parents forbade Kathy from dating Richard based entirely on the color of his skin and the constructed system of beliefs about Black men that have been perpetuated by a White dominant society. First, describing interracial marriage as potentially unbiblical was a concept based on a long-standing misinterpretation of passages from the Hebrew Bible in which God forbade Israelites from marrying into other people groups. The misinterpretation justified and excused racist thought with scripture. Second, the parents justified their response by claiming that interracial dating would be difficult for both Richard and Kathy as they would face racism as a couple. Although there is truth to this claim, it is not justification to forbid Kathy and Richard from dating.

**Disruption:** At the time of the conversation, James was unaware of systemic racism, but he knew that the decision was unjust and biased. He defended Richard's character and noted that he would treat his sister with a great deal of respect. James also openly disagreed with his parents' theological justification and conclusion that the two should not date because they might face racism from others. While James did not outright call his parents racist, he implied that they were acting as such.

As an aside, either James's parents' beliefs about interracial dating evolved or their perspective on interracial marriage and dating applied to only Black people, because he ended up marrying a person of color and his parents never protested. Their lack of protest could have been because James was an adult and they knew there was nothing they could really do to forbid him, but they treated his wife and her family with respect.

## "What about Black on Black Crime?"

This final scenario is from a Facebook post of a colleague of ours after the death of Alton Sterling. Because it is a transcript from a social media site, it differs in format from the previous examples: online interaction elicits different types of communication and engagement. Although this exchange did not occur around the Thanksgiving table, communicating via social media is becoming a different kind of table. In online spaces like Facebook, it is increasingly difficult to attempt real dialogue. As a result, this particular interaction is both poignant and incredibly instructive. Although the entire conversation is not posted here because dozens of people became involved in commenting, liking, and responding, the most in depth clips from the interaction are presented verbatim.

**Monica J—— feeling exhausted.**

July 6 at 10:50 am

A note of advice for my well-meaning White friends and associates. Today is not a day to debate race and police brutality with your friends of color, specifically those that are Black. We may not know Alton Sterling personally, but we know these circumstances and this feeling extremely well. This sense of fear and violation has been implanted in our psyche for centuries. As far back as the slave trade, slave hunters, lynchings, unleashed dogs, burnings, rapes, assaults … We as a people have been afraid to BE.

I live in constant fear … You probably haven't noticed because I work very hard to hide it. I fear for my life, my husband's life, my family in other states, my students … I am most anxiously afraid about the prospect of having black babies. I am scared to be put in the position to lose or explain this type of loss to my babies.

So today, I don't have it in me to teach you, model for you, perform for you. I'm not up for the thrill of a spirited debate. These ain't just words and fun conversations for me. This is a real life that I'm struggling every single day just to live. I do not currently possess the emotional fortitude, nor should you expect me to.

If you want to change the problem, figure out what you can do to fix a culture that allows for the continued murder of black and brown bodies without consequence. Figure out why certain agencies are overrun with individuals with problematic past and ideologies of race. Figure out how you can work to dismantle racism and its perpetuation in dominantly White communities.

Today … While we figure out once again how to love ourselves past fear, pain, and hopelessness … Work on you and yours.

#StopKillingUs #BlackLivesMatter #AltonSterling #WorkOnYou

Responder: I totally agree with you. I am white and I am afraid for myself, husband and children. They should go to jail for murder. Period. But during the last year I just have a question for Black Lives Matter? Why not put all the energy into the communities that have an overwhelming crime rate on Black on Black murders?? It's just a question don't cuss me out or call me names. Just asking. I know a lot of people have the same question? It always seems to be for racism.

Monica J——

I am not going to cuss you out or call you names.... I am confused as to why you would assume that name-calling and cursing would be the automatic response in this instance. This question however is case and point of the overall purpose of my original point ... I am not interested in debating with you. I would prefer not to have to break down years of knowledge and research on topics like implicit bias, the systematic disenfranchisement of people of color, the building of poverty, the confinement of people of color to targeted and purposefully under resourced areas, and so on and so forth.

I would suggest you do your own comprehensive research. I would suggest you research the overall efforts of the Black Lives Matter movement and their organizers. Deray Mckissick (one of the leaders) is actually extremely instrumental in community change in Baltimore. I would suggest you research what people of color do in their own communities. I am confident that there is a plethora of knowledge to be found. I however shall not take on the responsibility of providing it for you. Have a wonderful day.

Responder:

Thank you…If you knew me personally you would know I'm not racist at all. I have more black friends than white. I hate the police and I've seen my share of police brutality and it pisses me off. They abuse their power and it needs to stop. I worry everyday for my own family from the over reacting police. If the wall of racism could be torn down I believe we could help each other.

Monica J——

I understand that you may have approached this situation with the best of intentions. I would like to offer a legitimate explanation for the reception you are receiving. Please accept this in the manner it is given.

1) After I sincerely asked in my post for my well-intentioned white friends and associates to not attempt to enter into a debate on this day and around this subject, you followed up with

just that. Your question posted at this very moment, was offered up to begin a debate. I and probably all of the Black folks you know are tired and triggered. Now wasn't the time and this post wasn't the place.

2) Your question is considered a deflection, meaning it shifts the conversation away from a legitimate epidemic of police violence against Black folks to a conversation that has been long since debunked. Black on Black crime is a creation by majority powers, in the way that there is very little difference in the rate of Black people killing black people and white people killing white people or Asian people killing Asian people. The reality is that historically black people have been pathologized and you have been conditioned to be more critical of statistics that criminalize Black folks.

3) The manner you approached the situation is considered a microaggression. I would suggest you read the work of Dr. Derald Wing Sue. You essentially invalidated Black pain by ignoring a request to not engage by directly engaging and then suggesting the anger of pain was misplaced in suggesting that Black Lives Matters (i.e., Black folks) should really be mad at themselves for the circumstances that they live under.

4) You committed an additional microaggression by assuming that my response to you would be to cuss you or call you names. I am unsure why you would assume that I, who doesn't know you, would directly curse you or treat you poorly. It appears that you entered this situation with a preconceived expectation of me...Relying on a history of prejudice, I can only assume you thought I would be an angry black woman.

5) Having Black friends does not absolve you from the ability to have implicit bias or function within a system of racism. These things are not mutually exclusive. This is yet another form of microaggression. I hope that you are truly as interested in changing the world as you suggest that you are. If you would truly like to be an ally in this struggle or anyone else's, please reflect on what I have said here and look into the resources I

have suggested. Recognize that for me to write this response to you, I have had to try really hard to put my pain and anxiety to the side to provide education for you. Recognize that this has cost me something. Be blessed.

## A Way Forward

Perhaps we have all had similar situations in the past with friends and family and many of us may remain conflicted over what to do. Although we might desperately want to dismiss and write off people who believe this way, it also feels as divisive and dismissive as the racist friends and loved ones themselves if we walk away from our friends now. Ending these conversations by retreating to our own corner, or worse, ending relationships over philosophical differences, cannot and should not be the answer.

We encourage readers to think long term and to not walk away from the conversation or the relationship. Listen and seek to understand how and why they might think the way they do, and, most of all, stay in relationship with them. Although their views likely will not change overnight, our only hope is that they will open their eyes to different perspectives slowly over time. Kerry Ann Rockquemore[1], a frequent writer on the Inside Higher Education periodical's career section (entitled 'Dear Kerry Ann'), posted an article in response to a question about what she refers to as dreaded hallway conversations—informal discussions among colleagues that occur outside of the classroom, department meetings, or any other formal gathering where one might have prepared statements. Her four-point response, which we have modified and engage with below, offers much to consider for individuals who often feel ill equipped to engage in dreaded conversations in hallways or at Thanksgiving dinner.

### 1. Know Where You Stand and What You Want

Take time to figure out how you feel, identify your positions, and understand why you hold them. Take an inventory of what positions you hold close, where you are still unclear, and what positions you are afraid of not being able to defend to someone with strong contrasting views. Regardless of where you fall on a spectrum, be aware of your beliefs and where to draw your boundaries. Develop the skills to do so in a consistent and winsome manner that does not harm the relationships you value.

## 2. Be Open to Possibilities

We tend to dread certain conversations because we have already created a negative story about how that event will unfold. As such, we should consider that conversations on sensitive topics have the potential to take many different directions, including a nonexistent discussion, a combative argument, a conversation that leads to genuine interest, or even a transformative experience. When we walk into spaces and are open to the possibility that our colleagues, friends, or family members have grown and evolved over time, we may be surprised by the range of conversations that occur, allowing us to shift our attention to the fruitful ones, while drawing clear boundaries when the negative ones occur.

## 3. Learn What Healthy Dialogue Looks Like

Sometimes in our conversations, especially in difficult conversations, we can experience a range of conflicts, problems, occasional arguments, and silence. Good communication practices can lead to healthy dialogue where we are honest with each other and do not hide or sugarcoat true opinions or feelings. Learning and practicing the skills of nonviolent communication will enhance our ability to have healthy conflict and engage others in a winsome manner that maintains integrity while (sometimes necessarily) watering down our passion for a given topic.

## 4. Be Able to Separate People from Their Positions

Many relationships with friends and family are long-term commitments that are not easily severed without significant consequences

While a fear of burning relational bridges with loved ones should not drive our actions, we argue that it is important to stay at the proverbial table and work through issues with a long-term goal of reconciliation in mind. How might we continue to cultivate relationships with loved ones while holding loosely to their positions with which you disagree? Rockquemore argues that the ability to separate people from their positions is the hallmark of maturity and the foundation for long-term relationships. We can choose to dread and avoid difficult conversations and continue to ponder why little progress is made in race relations, or we can choose to engage in healthy and productive conflict on a regular basis.

## Conclusion

Given the nature and intent of this book, we focus on examples of White spaces and relationships in this chapter. Sometimes, White people who may consider themselves allies and advocates for racial justice might limit their relevant conversations to interactions with other people of color (seeking the ever gratifying and elusive Black Pat on the Back). However, when confronted by comments from family and friends of the same ethnicity, what do we do? Have we justified our silence by silently saying that we do this work by helping people of color at work? Or do we address issues with colleagues and rationalize saying nothing at home? This is the initial approach that I (Collins) had in my awakening stages of racial justice. Most conversations about issues of diversity occurred with other people of color; rarely with other white folks. I certainly did not engage family or long-time friends with these conversations. We are all searching for ways to navigate the right time, place, and words to engage and to disrupt the conversation patterns in our homogeneous spheres.

We acknowledge here that there is a collective frailty of the process of learning and communicating through difficult conversations. We are imperfect in our motivations and our attempts to dialogue; sometimes, we may find ourselves saying too much or too little. Learning how to do this right takes time and a great deal of practice. Given the final example about the Black on Black crime fallacy, we now turn to what it means to be a White ally and how to transform the role of dominance.

## Note

1. Rockquemore, Kerry Ann, "The dreaded hallway conversations," *Inside Higher Education*, last updated July 20, 2016, https://www.insidehighered.com/advice/2016/07/20/how-handle-conversations-over-crises-and-difficult-topics-news-essay

# Chapter Eight

# Good White Friends

## Written in Conjunction with Angie Hambrick and Joe Slavens

Much of what we have written has focused on our interactions and reflections with colleagues and friends around the country who have consistently defended dominance; readers who have made it thus far might wonder if there is a lack of hope. This thought is not our intent, and we do have hope. Our hope is based on knowing there is a way forward to racial reconciliation. Hope lies in the ability of friends in the dominant White majority to be part of the solution; advocates who use their places of privilege and positional authority regularly and who remain critically conscious and active toward racial justice.

The cumulative impact of White Pain, White 22, Whitefluenza, and deflections like Whitrogressions is ultimately a resounding defense of White dominance. There is a powerful force that operates in the White architecture of the mind that seeks to White Out that which may reveal the power of a system built on White logic. However, studies show that implicit bias can deconstructed. Even the U.S. Department of Justice mandated implicit bias training for the FBI, Drug Enforcement Administration, U.S. Marshalls, and U.S. attorneys, which have reached almost 30,000 federal personnel.[1] Such a wide reaching initiative de-

signed to engage large numbers of influencers is an indicator of movements to disentangle the way White dominance continues.

In the same vein, we conclude this book with our own study[2] designed to explore the experiences of White people within the United
States who have demonstrated a commitment to racial justice. Racial
justice activists, broadly defined, are individuals who work intentionally toward bringing about institutional and societal change.[3] Racial
Justice Allies, as noted in chapter four, are members of the dominant
group who seek to engage in activist work. As we are situated in universities, our study focused on White higher education administrators
who advocated for racial justice with an awareness of how their own
racial identities influenced their interactions with others in the midst of
change. All the participants worked in Dominantly White Institutions
and recognized individual and systemic racism as well as their own
positionality in institutional decision-making, policies, and climate for
students from subordinated backgrounds.[4] Social justice change agents
in higher education are committed to their own invidividual work of
deconstructing oppressive systems as well as empowering students to
engage in social change.

## Whiteness

Hegemony is "cultural power, including the dominant cultural patterns that achieve and sustain their dominance by encouraging—but
not forcing—people to believe in them."[5] Hegemonic Whiteness is an
identity that both produces and maintains domination through power and privilege.[6] Whiteness is internalized as normal and natural, in
turn marking non-Whites as abnormal and unnatural. Dominance and
subordination thus are sustained, not necessarily by force, but through
social practices, systems, and norms.[7] Systems of oppression are maintained because society does not challenge the validity of norms and
attitudes that perpetuate systems of domination and subordination because they are viewed as normal.

Peggy McIntosh's seminal definition of privilege was, "An invisible package of unearned assets which I can count on cashing in each

day, but about which I was meant to remain oblivious."[8] In the United States, Whiteness has afforded White people social and economic privileges that are not afforded to people of color. White people must be willing to accept that privilege is ensconced in the established systems to the detriment of people of color.[9] Furthermore, White people can break down oppressive systems by confronting White privilege as allies with people of color.

As long as White privilege is seen as invisible, the systems of oppression will continue to reinforce the social distance between Whites and racial minorities.[10] Dominant groups' members are granted unearned privileges based upon the perception that membership belongs to those who possess certain characteristics and values related to that particular social group.[11] (These unearned privileges are solely based on membership rather than merit, hard work, talent, or accomplishment.)

## White Identity Development

White identity development is a process that reflects the relationships between different social groups. Identity is conceptualized as a developmental construct that is defined by the understanding of self.[12] Healthy White identity is developed as individuals pass through particular stages and their attitudes toward White people and other racial/ethnic groups evolves and matures. The first steps toward positive White identity development involves understanding Whiteness, learning to accept Whiteness in relation to self, and internalizing a realistically positive view of what it means to identify as White.[13]

Janet Helms developed a model of White identity development and contended that "the evolution of a positive White racial identity consists of two processes, the abandonment of racism and the development of a non-racist White identity."[14] Framing White identity development in this fashion demonstrates the importance of the realization that racism affects not only those who are oppressed but also the oppressor. The abandonment of racism compels White individuals to acknowledge and understand their social, economic, and political positionality in a system based on White privilege and supremacy. In conjunction with abandoning racism, "he or she must accept his or her own Whiteness, the cultural implications of being White, and define a view of Self as a racial being that does not depend on the perceived superiority of one racial group."[15]

Although there are sound reasons that some scholars question Helms' model of stage progression of identity development, there is agreement that Helms' work accurately represents White racial consciousness. White people can either have an unachieved or achieved racial consciousness, but White identity development may be a more complex and complicated process than Helms originally asserted.

## Racial Justice Alliances

According Frances Kendall, allyship requires a great deal of self-examination as well as a willingness to initiate personal, institutional, and societal justice and equality.[16] The reasons people from privileged groups support social justice are varied and multifaceted. Common motivators include personal relationships with individuals from oppressed groups, the need to act morally, and discomfort with discrepancies between beliefs and the inequalities observed around them.

We submit that White critical consciousness is a mindfulness that allies have who work in, what Cipolle defined as, "solidarity with marginalized groups of social justice and mutual liberation."[17] There are three stages of White critical consciousness. The initial stage, *charity*, is marked by individuals who may have had limited exposure to people of color but engage in service to help others because it is the "right thing to do." The emerging stage is *caring*. Individuals in this stage experience the dissonance of what they believed to be true and the new reality they are beginning to construct because of their service. White students begin to develop empathy, not sympathy, for the communities they are serving. The developing stage of White critical consciousness for students engaging in service-learning is *social justice*. Individuals make an ongoing commitment to working in allyship with various communities and "need to understand the connection between power and knowledge and recognize how power is used in coercive ways to control society and control individuals in body, mind, and spirit."[18] Cipolle's model demonstrated the ongoing and continuous development of White individuals as they work towards social justice and change.

## Critical Race Theory

We framed our study around the tenets of Critical Race Theory (CRT),[19] which derived from critical legal studies and civil rights activists in the 1970s, and our work around Critical White Studies (CWS). Both of these approaches are central conceptual frameworks that guided our study. CRT scholars examine the intersections of race, racism, and power.[20] Racism has become pervasive, constant, and ingrained in established structures, but dominant populations often do not recognize or acknowledge racism's reality. Critics argue that because racism is so pervasive, it is often not recognized or acknowledged, leading to denial and inaction. This lack of acknowledgment can lead to the denial and inaction that is an aspect of White privilege, which is a key proposition of CWS.

Although there are several basic tenets of CRT, we concentrated on one component for this study. In addition to being an everyday occurrence, racism is "the usual way society does business, the common, everyday experience of most people of color in this country."[21] CRT takes the stance that racism and White privilege are critical in creating the system of dominance and subordination that is deeply rooted in our society. CRT promotes a more complete discourse about race and "a fuller appreciation of the real meanings of 'race', one that helps us confront the ways in which 'race' continue to disable us all."[22]

In reference to Critical White Studies, Delgado and Stefancic explained that the discipline of CWS seeks to understand what it means to be White, in addition to the legal privileges, power, and supremacy that are all embedded in racial dominance. Ultimately, White people must be willing to accept that their privilege is engrained in all systems in order to actively work in cooperation and in allyship with people of color to break down oppressive systems. Just as CRT begins with questioning the pervasiveness of race and the social, economic, and political construction of race, another tenet of CWS challenges the normativity and invisibility of Whiteness in the dialogues and research around race.

## The Study

We were looking for an answer to the question: What characterizes White folks in higher education who choose to engage in social justice and diversity work? Racial justice is defined as moving "beyond mere appreciation or celebration into active efforts to examine and dismantle oppressive structures and policies and move toward a more equitable vision for the institution and its members."[23] In this study, we analyzed the experiences of nine White administrators who were nominated by peers as having a strong commitment to social justice and engaged in consistent behaviors and activities.

The following descriptions of these participants' journeys toward a social justice consciousness reflects an iterative process of interaction with individuals who set into motion a desire for more awareness of diversity, social justice, and difference. Participants were able to sustain their commitment to racial justice and action because of the strong alliances they developed. Exploring the meanings of power and privilege as well as engaging other White people in their own personal journey of racial justice consciousness also marked the participants of our study. Critical consciousness as depicted in Figure 8.1 is an iterative and interconnected cyclical process. The process begins with individuals having a deeply personal and meaningful critical moment with an activator, but it never ends there. These interactions raise the level of awareness about issues of difference and cause dissonance. Individuals on the road to critical consciousness move beyond essentializing and exoticizing the other, and take action to explore their own privilege and the systems of subordination that effect individuals with multiple identities (e.g. race, class, religion). The persistent aspiration to engage in racial justice encourages individuals in this framework to advocate, on behalf and in solidarity with others. Along the way, the new alliances they form, both in their own identity groups as well in groups they do not have membership, create additional challenges and greater awakenings in their journey as change agents, generating even

greater introspection and propelling them forward in the cycle of critical consciousness. The model helps to explain the inter-relatedness of
the elements of the White journey to becoming an ally. The stages do
not always and perhaps rarely move in a precise cycle and the stages
intersect frequently. This model serves to document the experiences of
our participants as they continued the ongoing process of solidifying
a social justice advocate identity. The model also illustrates the process
of critical consciousness that may be used by White friends to create
programs, services, and spaces for other White advocates who choose
to engage in the process of critical consciousness.

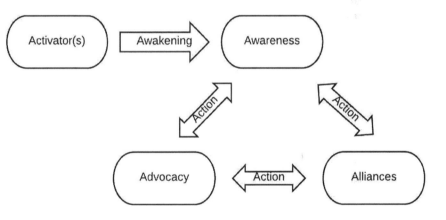

Figure 8.1. Cycle of Consciousness

## Activators, Awakening, and Awareness

All participants in our study pointed to an interaction with a person,
an activator, who was racially or culturally different than themselves
as a defining moment in their journey to social justice consciousness.
Trisha and Karen's initial feelings of incongruence with what they were
taught in their families began to diminish as they continued to immerse
themselves in other cultures and ways of knowing.

Karen shared her family history of involvement with the Ku Klux
Klan and how that history of racist ideology framed her understanding of people of color. However, Karen pointed to her interactions with

a Black man named Roosevelt who worked in her town as a formative experience. She shared how her family's racism was "framed by dad's understanding, and so that was a part of the understanding that I had, but I had no other frame to work with to change that until I met Roosevelt." Karen's relationship with Roosevelt was her awakening, because she realized despite the Klan's teachings of racial intolerance and hate, that "this is a person just like me." Trisha's awakening happened during her 10 years of service in Europe. She began to notice that her "traditional, conservative evangelical" ways of knowing and expressing her faith was a different expression than the individuals she was working with overseas.

William and Steven grew up with best friends who were racially different than them. William's best friend growing up was a Latino boy named Carlos. He said,

> his family was like a second family for me and I saw some of the challenges he experienced as a person of color. So I think that was a powerful statement for me at an early age and really seeing this isn't the way it should be.

While William began to recognize these differences based on race early in his relationship with Carlos, Steven did not notice these differences in his relationship with Sharon, his best friend, who was Black. Steven described Sharon as,

> mixed race, her mother was Irish, but her father was African American with some Japanese. So if you looked at her, your first impression of her would be somewhat light skinned but African American female. And she was probably my closest friend in high school. Now for me, she was just Sharon. I didn't think twice about her race.

Steven's recognition of Sharon as a person of color eventually occurred when he transferred to a school that was more homogenous and White. He reflected,

> coming from a more diverse high school, we had, like I said, Latinos and Hispanics there, I had an African American friend or two, to this place where it was like all middle class White kids and it was so not my scene, I guess.

For Steven, being in an environment where there were less people who resembled his best friend Sharon began to trigger recognition of differences and how Sharon would have to struggle in order to fit in and be accepted into such an environment.

Bruce did not necessarily have direct interactions with individuals who were culturally and racially different from him, but he lived in environments and countries that made difference difficult to ignore. These environments made clear that suffering and injustice were a reality for subordinated groups. Bruce's parents worked in a depressed, urban area in South America. He recalls some memories of his ten years in that country: "The sight of beggars on the streets with open wounds, and discover[ing] that some were legitimately struggling, and homeless." In this case, witnessing people who were homeless was a catalyst for Bruce's deeper reflection on the impacts of racism and classism that he would later explore in his adult life.

Jamie and Frank's interactions with others helped them to recognize the different lived realities of individuals. Jamie recalled a Black man who worked for her grandfather and who dined with the family; this memory was her first recollection of recognizing racial difference. She reflected that the man was no different than her grandfather – he worked hard to support his family just as her grandfather. Frank spoke of volunteerism as one way he began to put a face to injustice:

> I would say that opportunities that I had growing up, like specifically opportunities when I was kind of "volun-told," to do volunteer service, mandatory service in high school or in college ... those are opportunities that I had that I think really put a face to the vulnerable ...

Activators are individuals who exposed our participants to diversity and difference. However, these interactions with difference were not enough to create a social justice consciousness. In additions to these interactions with others, the participants experienced a critical moment that necessitated learning or reframing knowledge from their dominant identity categories (race, ethnicity, socio-economic standing) into a greater understanding and empathy for individuals with subordinated group identities.

# Alliances

Participants were able to deepen their understanding of their own privilege and to persist in their journeys toward social justice consciousness through creating and sustaining meaningful relationships or alliances with people with historically marginalized identities. These relationships were rooted in both the participants' own sense of personal responsibility to their emerging social justice self and to others who were affected by systems of oppression as well as in a deep commitment to their faith and religious values.

The participants in this study made numerous references to the personal responsibility they felt to engage in social justice and change. They referred to social justice as work that needs to be done. All recognized that as individuals with privilege it was their responsibility to build alliances, to work in coalition with others to dismantle systems of oppression, and to engage other privileged individuals in the work.

Eric and William both spoke about their new awareness of social injustices as impossible to "turn it off." Eric said, "I see so much that needs to be done and I feel in some ways embarrassed and in some ways just frustrated, like why can't we do more? Why is this not coming together?" William also spoke about his frustrations with other White people:

> Even as a [resident hall director], I would often plan programs that really talked about inclusion and the importance of multiculturalism. And whenever I would do that I would notice that it was me and a lot of African American students or Latino students or Latina students. And that always bothered me that there wasn't a broader sense of the importance of those conversations.

Eric and William felt a sense of personal responsibility to build alliances with others in order to increase their understanding of social justice and inclusion.

Elizabeth, who adopted a child of color from another country, spoke about the personal and professional responsibilities she felt for social justice engagement:

I am now more aware of things, but not just [fully] aware … I now have a different responsibility to engage … This is kind of hard, but the journey is the
engagement.

The participants continued to build alliances with others out of personal responsibility to continue their own journey to social justice consciousness but also to engage others on the journey as well.

## Advocacy

While each of our participants had one critical moment or interaction
with an individual who had at least one subordinate identity that was
different than their own, they continued beyond this moment to further
their journey with social justice. They persisted and continued to engage difference in two ways. First, the participants continued to grapple with White privilege; second, they wanted to engage other White
people in these conversations.

Validating the stories of others was a necessary component in the
experiences of the participants. In order for a critical moment to be
more than a chance encounter with an "other" or an activator, participants had to discern the moment or the story of that individual and in-
ternalize it. Although participants gained insight into the experiences
of others through critical moments, it took intentional reflection and
time for each participant to recognize how oppression is systemic and
not just the isolated experiences of the other with whom they have a
relationship. Eric shared,

> I cared about these people and thought, that doesn't fit, I don't understand
> why they have to go through that. So over time, being humbled myself and re-
> alizing if I'm a White male who actually has a certain amount of opportunity, I
> need to use my voice, whatever voice God chooses to give me to advocate for
> those who don't have that voice.

After recognizing that the stories of others are valid, participants began
to confront privilege and how their access to unearned benefits, social
standings, and rights were incongruent with their emerging social justice consciousness.

Awareness and recognition of power and privilege also marked participants' ability to move beyond their critical moment. A number of participants noted a commitment to identifying privilege and thinking critically about what they can do with access to privilege, not in pity but in solidarity with subordinated groups. Steven reflected on his White privilege in the following way: "I get the shorter line for no particular reason other than I've been pre-selected in a category that is arbitrary. That gives me certain obligations or responsibilities perhaps to use that privilege wisely."

Elizabeth reflected on her time in South America where she worked in communities in high poverty. She remembered not having access to clean water, a place to sleep at night, and other luxuries typical of her home life in the United States, but she looked forward to her trip to that village every year for five years. She reflected on this experience:

> I just couldn't wait until my next opportunity to go back ... to this place that didn't have you know, access to clean water or food, didn't have access to education, was extremely violent. I can look back in retrospect and say, well, I was so excited to go back and engage for this variety of reasons and I always got to come home afterwards and I always got to come back to my clean water and abundance of food and my good education and my nice, warm home ... And so I think that was maybe a defining experience in terms of coming to um, understanding issues about access and privilege.

Elizabeth's time in South America helped her to understand privilege and to grapple with its implications. Another participant, Eric, sought to use his privilege:

> I realize that what can help me and keep me humble is that I have a lot of blind spots. I can realize that I just don't get it. I now have the opportunity to be an influence for change because of the authority and privilege I have. I have privilege but not all the answers; I try to listen well and advocate for others.

Frank and William both mentioned White and male privilege in the context of their professional lives and the obligations they have to use privilege to dismantle oppressive systems. Frank said,

As a straight White male who is director to one of the largest areas at our school, I have privilege. I have access to students, and I'm passionate about identifying the need for an intercultural dialogue. I've been able to leverage our fiscal resources to bring in speakers regarding intercultural competence and dialogue.

Frank leverages his status as a director, as well as his access to resources, to advocate for intercultural dialogue and leadership opportunities.

William called privilege "the air we breathe, and it's all we know" and shared that conversations about privilege are beginning to take place on his campus. He reflected on the very privileged environment he works in—higher education in general and his institution specifically—but admitted that he has to remind himself daily about the privileged environment he works in. He takes his environment for granted because,

> I can afford to. I don't have to consciously think about my environment. I'm not the minority or fearful for safety, or I don't have to wonder what that faculty member means when she asks that particular question. I'm trying to become more and more aware of privilege.

The participants' dedication motivated them to reflect on their own privilege and how they perpetuate systems of domination and subordination because of their own dominant identity categories. William stressed the point that everyone at his institution should be involved in racial justice work: it is not just the responsibility of an office of multicultural affairs or people of color to be the loudest voice. He said, "They are not to be the only ones to speak up about these issues, so I try to speak up as a White senior level administrator."

The findings offer implications for how White college administrators may support one another in social justice education and advocacy endeavors and illuminates a better understanding of the experiences of White administrators from institutions who are purported to engage in social justice programs, activities, and initiatives. In turn, these White administrators may become role models for students to begin their own journeys toward becoming social justice advocates. The findings are also transferrable to White people seeking to be allies working in White dominant environments.

## Space for White Identity Formation

The capacity for White identity formation cannot be left to chance. Spaces must be created for White people to have conversations about "what it means to be white, how whiteness became established legally, the phenomenon of white power and white supremacy, and the group of privileges that comes with membership in the dominant race."[24] White privilege depends on the intentional or unintentional domination of people of color. White people must be willing to accept that their privilege is engrained in all systems in order to actively work in cooperation and in allyship with people of color to break down oppressive systems.

The participants all spoke about the importance of a critical "light bulb" moment with an individual with racial and class identities that were different than their own. However, participants also spoke about the importance of sharing new knowledge of social justice issues, their own privilege, and ways to combat oppressive systems with other White people. White individuals who have a commitment to social justice and are active advocates for social change find it difficult to share their experiences as social justice allies with other Whites. They perceive their motives and desire for social change as unconventional and not accepted by other Whites, so they may keep their views and actions private. Thus, it is important for White individuals who are invested in social change to have social support and spaces where honest dialogue about their views about power and privilege can be expressed. Multiple spaces, homogenous and cross-cultural, are a need for White identity development.

## Cycle of Critical Consciousness

The Cycle of Critical Consciousness (Figure 8.1) depicts interaction with activators, an awakening and greater awareness of issues of racial justice in inequity, and building alliances for appropriate advocacy in collaboration with subordinated communities. This model demonstrates that racial justice and change is the responsibility of all individuals in society. It is possible through critical reflection, authentic leadership, and cultural humility, to become an agent of change.

The aim of this narrative study was to give voice to a population of White educators awakening to privilege and systemic racism in college and, by extension, broader society. Our hope is that by documenting and learning of their journeys toward racial justice consciousness, more educators will come to a sober understanding of the experiences and challenges of racial justice endeavors, including justice advocates and allies. Our hope is that this chapter, and indeed the entire book, can serve to inform and challenge other White educators who do not currently view racism as still being a problem. We hope that more readers would ultimately find themselves as both part of the problem but also an integral part of the solution. This is our call for all those longing for change to be emboldened in their efforts to make a positive difference in their immediate communities. We hope to use our privilege intentionally in our various spheres of influence to create a more just and racially equitable society.

## Notes

1. Department of Justice Announces New Department Wide Implicit Bias Training for Personnel (June 27 2016). https://www.justice.gov/opa/pr/department-justice-announces-new-department-wide-implicit-bias-training-personnel

2. An earlier version of this paper was presented at the professional conference. Slavens, Joe, Angelica Hambrick, Alexander Jun, Mari Luna De La Rosa, Sharia Brock, and Jake Gilbertson, *Narrative Tales of Social Justice Engagement*, presented at the Association of the Study of Higher Education (ASHE), November 2014 (Washington, DC).

3. Edwards, Keith E. "Aspiring social justice ally identity development: A conceptual model." *NASPA Journal* 43, no. 4 (2006): 39–60.

4. Davis, Lori Patton, Marylu McEwen, Laura Rendon, and Mary Howard-Hamilton. "Critical race perspectives on theory in student affairs." (2007).

5. Parker, Robert Dale. *Critical theory: A reader for literary and cultural studies*. Oxford: Oxford University Press, 2012.

6. Hughey, Matthew W. "The (dis) similarities of white racial identities: The conceptual framework of 'hegemonic whiteness'." *Ethnic and Racial Studies* 33, no. 8 (2010): 1289–1309.

7. McClaren, Peter. "Critical pedagogy: A look at the major concepts," *The critical pedagogy reader,* eds. Darder, Antonia, Marta Baltodano, and Rodolfo D. Torres (Hove UK: Psychology Press, 2003), 61–83.

8. McIntosh, Peggy, White Privilege, and Male Privilege. *A personal account of coming to see correspondences through work in women's studies.* Working Paper 189, Center for Research on Women, Wellesley College, Wellesley, MA, 1988. Retrieved February 1, 2010, from http://www. nymbp. org/reference/WhitePrivilege. pdf, 1988.

9. Lipsitz, George. *The possessive investment in whiteness: How white people profit from identity politics.* Philadelphia, PA: Temple University Press, 2006.

10. Hays, Danica G., and Catherine Y. Chang. "White privilege, oppression, and racial identity development: Implications for supervision." *Counselor Education and Supervision* 43, no. 2 (2003): 134–146.

11. Lechuga, Vicente M., Laura Norman Clerc, and Abigail K. Howell. "Power, privilege, and learning: Facilitating encountered situations to promote social justice." *Journal of College Student Development* 50, no. 2 (2009): 229–244.

12. Torres, Vasti, Susan R. Jones, and Kristen A. Renn. "Identity development theories in student affairs: Origins, current status, and new approaches."*Journal of College Student Development* 50, no. 6 (2009): 577–596.

13. Reason, Robert Dean, Elizabeth A. Roosa Millar, and Tara C. Scales. "Toward a model of racial justice ally development." *Journal of College Student Development* 46 no. 5 (2005): 530–546.

14. Helms, Janet E. *Black and White racial identity: Theory, research, and practice.* Santa Barbara, CA: Greenwood Press, 1990, 49.

15. Ibid.

16. Kendall, Frances. *Understanding white privilege: Creating pathways to authentic relationships across race.* New York: Routledge, 2012.

17. Cipolle, Susan Benigni. *Service-learning and social justice: Engaging students in social change.* New York: Rowman & Littlefield Publishers, 2010, 63.

18. Ibid., p. 62.

19. We acknowledge several scholars who have paved the way for our work, including Derrick Bell (see Bell, Derrick A. "Who's afraid of critical race theory." *U. Ill L. Rev.* (1995): 893) and Delgado and Stefancic (see Delgado, Richard, and Jean Stefancic. *Critical race theory: An introduction.* New York: NYU Press, 2012); Gloria Ladson Billings (see Ladson-Billings, Gloria. "Just what is critical race theory and what's it doing in a nice field like education?." *International Journal of Qualitative Studies in Education* 11, no. 1 (1998): 7–24); and Daniel Solórzano (see Lynn, Marvin, Tara J. Yosso, Daniel G. Solórzano, and Laurence Parker. "Critical race theory and

education: Qualitative research in the new millennium." *Qualitative Inquiry* 8, no. 1 (2002): 3–6.).

20. Delgado, Richard, and Jean Stefancic. *Critical race theory: An introduction.* New York: NYU Press, 2012.

21. Ibid., p. 7.

22. Valdes, Francisco, Jerome McCristal Culp, and Angela Harris. *Crossroads, directions and a new critical race theory.* Philadelphia: PA: Temple University Press, 2002, 182.

23. Thompson, Candace, Sheri Hardee, and James C. Lane. "Engaging student diversity through a Social Justice Learning Community." *Journal of Diversity in Higher Education* 4, no. 2 (2011): 106, 112.

24. Delgado, Richard, and Jean Stefancic. *Critical race theory: An introduction.* New York: NYU Press, 2012, 83.

# Chapter Nine

# Conclusion: A Way Forward

We recently watched a seminar by Joy DeGruy Leary on Post Traumatic Slave Syndrome in London.[1] At one point in her seminar, DeGruy Leary asked the audience to raise their hands if they believe in White racism and again if they believe in Black racism. As hands stayed still, moved up, or moved slowly halfway up, the room became tense. Dr. DeGruy Leary then asked the participants how they could know the effects of White racism. Some of the answers included inequalities in education, healthcare, and other areas. She went on to ask how they can know the effects of Black racism. The room fell silent and she explained the silence is due to the fact that power makes White racism have pervasive and real effects. Conversely, Black racism often carries some layers of disdain and even hate, but does not have the influence on the ability to get a loan or even incarceration rates. She explained that the only influence Black racism carries is fear. White people are afraid of Black people. It is deeply psychological. Norm Stamper's work revealed the extreme version of this fear among police officers.[2] The bigger and darker the Black man, the more extreme the level of fear.

I (Collins) enjoy stand up paddle boarding in the Pacific Ocean. Spaces inhabited by people are inherently racialized—deserts to oceans and suburbs to wilderness. A warm day at the beginning of the Summer of 2016, as I came upon the sand, I saw a mother and young boy watching me emerge out of the cool pacific ocean. The beach was empty except for the two of them. It is always a potential scene when there are waves because it requires good timing to get in and out of the water. I smiled, picked up my board and started walking toward the road where I was parked. On the way, I passed a large Black man. As he passed, we exchanged a nod and kept walking. When he was about 20 feet behind me and headed down a path to the beach, he turned around and began to jog back toward me. I saw him coming and bristled, tense, blood pumping, internal caution flags flying. I tried to act like I was not experiencing fear. I do not remember exactly what he asked, but it was related to some curiosity he had about my paddleboard and a recounting of how he and his family were watching me paddle from the beach. I went back to the truck and loaded the board and sat down with ice water running through my veins wondering *why*. How has this fear been so deeply woven into the White psyche?

I (Jun) grew up admiring and paradoxically fearing adolescent White boys. As a shy, overweight, sixth grader who moved from one dominantly White elementary school to an equally dominantly White middle school in northern California, I was bullied regularly by a few of my Black and mostly White classmates. The Black boys were seen as disruptive both inside and outside of class, and everyone, including all of my White teachers, seemed to fear the Black boys. However unlike the Black boys, the White boys were popular and well liked by both students and teachers. Blond haired, blue-eyed, athletic and clean cut, they were well spoken, polite to teachers, coaches, and administrators. I recall most of them attending catechism classes on Wednesdays or went to temple on Saturdays. Only recently had I realized how much many of them look like my co-author. In fact, many of the young White boys resembled characters I would see on television in the 1980's. Again, I admired them from a distance and recall trying to emulate their speech, mannerisms, and actions. However, I was taken aback and dismayed, heartbroken really, when these popular and handsome young White boys began to tease me and make fun of my hair, my eyes, and my yellow skin. Microaggressive comments toward me in class, as well as outright racial insults verbalized in class, went unnoticed by my White teachers who had proven their ability to hear every other inappropriate word uttered in class. I felt heartbroken and betrayed, and I wondered why people in authority did nothing to stop the pain I felt. I was not able to put into words, at the time, the systemic nature of it all. White boys who were popular had a dark side to them, known only to a handful of select minority students; teachers who represented power and authority in my life were silent in the face of racial injustice. Whenever I see young clean-cut adolescent White boys, I still feel that sense of distrust and recognize my own implicit biases toward them.

Although the individual experience is important, we have tried to create a vocabulary for understanding the White system in a new way. In doing so, we did not intend to provide a set of rules by which someone can confirm their status as a nice White person. We do not believe there is a set of rules to follow that will generate consciousness and acceptance. We are, however, convinced of the existence of a pervasive White system that can be seen, in part, through self-examination. Individual examination should not obscure the role of the system and its influence over mental architecture.

One example of the global nature of this system are the layers of Whiteness seen in various cultures. Most systems of racial hierarchy are built around color, and lighter skin is almost always at the top. In subsequent volumes, we plan to explore the religious and global nature of the system. One religious text (paraphrased) states that people who hear something and don't act or respond are like those who look in the mirror and quickly forget what they look like. We have found that privilege affords us the ability to hear something and forget it, to be confronted with inequity and act for a time, but ultimately to take a break if we need to. The confluence of virus-like privilege, the resistance to hear the pain of others, feigning offence, feeling paralyzed, and staying angry are a stronghold of defense for White dominance. We hope that by seeing it, examining it, acknowledging it, and facilitating discussion around it, we can approach consciousness raising. We hope to become new architects of our own minds and encourage others to the same.

We know that for many readers the chapters included herein have elicited strong reactions and times of stretching. Our intent was to not only bring new language to longstanding ideas, but also to help transform some of the tired conversations you engage in regularly regarding racial justice. Undoubtedly, there are some who have found much of this content to be quite challenging. We appreciate all who have traveled this journey with us.

For those who might turn away and disengage, never to return to these conversations again, who have been turned off by the way the writing has made you feel due to our inability to convey a clearer more winsome message, we express our regrets. However, for those who have experienced a transformation in thinking and a fresh new perspective to engage in the conversation, we submit that the real work of reconciliation begins now, with those around you in your communities—your college campuses, churches, synagogues, with co-workers, and especially beloved friends and family, even during Thanksgiving.

The time has come to be bold and courageous. Despite the temptations to give up and give in, we must persevere. When the work is too much, the journey too long, and the conflicts too difficult, the time has come for peace and reconciliation. We can. We must.

## Notes

1. DeGruy Leary, Joy. *Post traumatic slave disorder*, Retrieved February 18, 2014 https://www.youtube.com/watch?v=XRQ-Ci6LwVw
2. Stamper, Norm. *Breaking rank: A top cop's expos of the dark side of American policing*, New York: Nation Books, 2009.

# Definitions

These definitions are from *White Out* (Collins & Jun, 2017).

*White Out*, the action of intentional or unintentional blotting, serves the purpose of trying to obscure others experiences in lieu of a competing definition of reality.

The *White architecture of the mind* is a term and an analogy to highlight that the mind is a result of a set of blueprints, constructions, walls, doors, windows, and pathways that influence and predispose individuals to react based on a systemic logic that was socially constructed.

*White pain* is a pattern of how White folks either unwittingly or with passive aggressive defense strategies place their own pain in the foreground of a discussion to the exclusion and erasure of pain that racialized others face.

*White-upping* is a defense mechanism where White people, uncomfortable with stories of racism from People of Color, steal pain and begin disclosing their own individual pain.

*Whitefluenza* is the notion that White privilege spreads, mutates, lies dormant, is more visible at various times due to acute symptoms, and is part of a larger system where members unwittingly change the rules or perspectives to maintain dominance.

*White 22*—the feeling of futility that White people feel when they are criticized or challenged while engaged in racial justice.

*Whitrogressions* are verbal slights, racial slurs, and insults toward White people that do not have the same power and magnitude as macro or microaggressions toward people of color, but are taken with the same level of offense.

*Angry White men* are not so much a group of people as it is a spreading sentiment around the world to recapture a sense of what has been lost—namely, dominant Whiteness.

# Index